DPH Education Series

COMPUTER EDUCATION

U K SINGH • K N SUDARSHAN

DISCOVERY PUBLISHING HOUSE
NEW DELHI-110002

Discovery Publishing House
4831/24, Ansari Road, Darya Ganj
New Delhi - 110 002 (INDIA)

Computer Education
Edition : 2006
Reprinted - 2014
ISBN 978-81-7141-356-0

PRINTED IN INDIA
Dynamic Printers, Delhi

Preface

The *DPH Education Handbook* has been created to provide access to information about contemporary topics in education. Practitioners and students at all levels in education have a need to know what is happening today, in addition to historical treatments within the literature.

Each chapter within the Handbook is designed to provide the user with needed "state-of-the-art" information as well as further sources of information. One of the significant features of each chapter is the inclusion of specific programmes, projects and activities so that the researcher can locate human resources as well as the literature.

The handbook will be of use to graduate and post graduate students in education and to practicing teachers, administrators, librarians and planners. The chapters and the further sources of information cited in each book should lead the reader to thousands of people and documents for either research or programme planning purposes.

An effort to achieve universal and effective education is based on a recognition of the rights of students to basic education that enables them to thrive in a complex society, as well as a realization the technological and economic growth is facilitated by increasing the numbers of students, even those with poor academic progresses, who are, in fact successful in learning. Thus, recent and current efforts improve education serve both private and social interests.

This series is addressed to administrators, planners and educators working in the field of education and training with a view to stimulating interest and attention in the areas of education and its related fields. It is also addressed to a growing number of teachers and instructors who will be practitioners in education and who will need to be acquainted with the modern aspects of educational practice and development. Many ideas, generalisations and discussions presented in this series should also prove useful to employing organisations committed to provide training facilities within their establishments—leading to effective mutual participation by institutions and organisations.

The editors wishes to thank the contributors, as well as those organizations that gave permission to publish their extracts, chapters etc.

Editors

Contents

	Preface	v
1.	Computer Literacy	1
2.	Computers in Education	41
3.	The Role of Computers in High-Order Thinking	102
4.	Computer-Based Learning	139
5.	Computers and the Organisation of Learning	202
6.	Computers and the Curriculum	231
7.	Computers and the Educational Programme	262
8.	Computer-Related Learning in Vocational Education	296
	Index	327

1 Computer Literacy

The term "Computer literacy" is little more than a decade old. In part because it is so new, it is a "humpty-dumpty" concept which can mean whatever its users want it to mean. Consequently, the literature abounds with diverse definitions of computer literacy and with varied descriptions of school programs for realizing it. Both the youthfulness of the concept and its heterogeneous meanings have import for those engaged in the study of educational policy.

In probing the "whiter literacy" question, three general but related outcomes will be sought. First, descriptions and analyses of current literacy concepts and programs are presented on the assumption that the status quo needs to be mapped before the "whither" question is addressed. Second, some of the deeply conflicting perspectives on computer uses are briefly delineated in order to highlight the controversies which surround literacy decisions. Third, a rationale for analyzing the "whither" question is explicated and used to probe paths into the future.

Several assumptions underline the ideas

presented in this chapter. First, the societal changes wrought by microelectronic technologies will have greater implications for changes in educational programs than will the instructional potential of these technologies. Second, since future scenarios about life in the developing computer culture will, in the final analyss, be written by individuals, the capacities of schools to enhance self-realization will become increasingly significant. Third, all of the important issues related to uses of microcomputers ultimately reside beyond technology in human and social domains. Finally, the objectives of computer literacy programs cannot be permanently fixed; they change as societal values and technology change.

The diverse meanings of computer literacy

At a general level, differences in the conceptual and practical meanings of computer literacy exist within and across nations, at a specific level, they are found in the multiple programs offered in given school. Diversity expresses itself through the scope and depth of computer literacy programs, the objectives they seeks, the outcomes they produce, and the places they occupy in curricula. Computer literacy programs now found in schools are not easy to classify, in part because they are usually defined in general terms. In addition, those describing programs often fail to distinguish clearly between concepts and their uses, and the resulting obscurities make classification difficult. Nevertheless, the categories of literacy elaborated below do help document and clarify the diverse expressions of current programs.

Operational literacy

Those who have acquired "operational" literacy can define the basic components of hardware and software and can demonstrate the machine-related skills needed to make computers work. Designed to introduce students to the computer, this approach is often implemented through daily exercises during a period of several weeks. When the exercises are effective, students understand such concepts as "monitor", "keyboard," and "central processing unit" and how the components labeled by such concepts work together with other parts to make computers function. Students are also able to turn a computer on and off, load software, show proficiency at the keyboard, demonstrate the use of storage devices, and acquire "minimal" troubleshooting techniques.

Operational literacy, then, emphasizes "hands on" experiences and simple concepts. Directed at elementary understandings and skills, the approach demands neither extensive teacher training nor substantial amounts of instructional time. Nor does it require much change in existing curricula or major investments beyond those made in hardware and software. The minimal demands of the approach may account for the fact that many school districts have opted for it in their initial literacy efforts. The approach, while limited, provides an entry into the world of the computer and a potential bridge to more significant learning experiences; more easily than other literacy alternatives, operational literacy can be made available equitably to all students.

Learning produced through operational literacy, critics argue, are both trivial and subject to quick obsolescence. They might contend, for example, that teaching students how to turn computers on and off is just as trivial as teaching them how to turn television sets on and off. Both activities squander valuable time. Critics also argue that operational literacy outcomes are immediately out of date, hardware and software are changing so fast, they say, that today's operations are obsolescent tomorrow. In addition, future computers, with their enhanced "friendliness," intelligence, and simplicity, will require only the most elementary skills. Why waste students' and teachers' time, critics ask, by providing trivial and obsolescent learnings?

Is the assumption about obsolescence as sound one? Since students of technology typically underestimate, often substantially, the time required to realize new developments, a note of skepticism is in order. Put differently, projections made about impending achievements in intelligent and friendly computers by critics of operational literacy, especially the highly optimistic ones, are likely to be in error. If the new technologies have potential for enhancing learning, then a pertinent question arises; why wait years for more powerful computers while immediately closing the door on opportunities for all students to acquire potentially useful entry skills and concepts?

Is the "triviality" argument sound? If the learnings acquired through operational literacy offer no foundation for new learnings, they can be classed as trivial . However, if the elementary and first-stage learnings facilitate the attainment of more advanced ones, they are not necessarily trivial. To be sure, research is needed to determine if the "operational" learnings acquired in fact enable students to realize more sophisticated learnings. Further, do students from diverse backgrounds actually use the initial learnings to acquire more advanced ones?

Instrumental literacy

In this approach to literacy computers are used as instruments for acquiring stipulated learnings or bodies of subject matter, In Sweden, for example, leaders have used computers in high schools to teach mathematics and civics. They chose these subjects in parts because they "are taken by all compulsory school pupils, and they are included in most lines of upper secondary school". The approach enables all enrolled students to learn to use computers as they acquire content or skills; in addition, the computer can be used as an instrument for "modernizing" subject-matter teaching. In the Swedish plan, for example, computer-supported projects produced, according to one observer, a variety of subject-related outcomes among which were new insights by students into mathematical relationships, into "connections" among subject matters, and into the analytical aspects of mathematics. In addition, teachers coordinated instruction in physics and mathematics more effectively.

The Swedish approach reflects the

instrumental use of computers in selected subjects. Some high school leaders have aspired to use computers in all subjects taught. Those taking clerical courses, for example, might acquire word processing skills; some social studies students, insights into environmental problems through simulations; science students, understandings of physics from computer-based demonstrations; language arts students, enhanced vocabulary and spelling skills, and so forth. In each subject, in other words, the computer would provide a tool for advancing learning.

The instrumental concept of computer literacy is not without its critics. Some detractors maintain that this alternative provides "low level" types of learning only. Others are skeptical about whether the quality of future software will exceed significantly that currently available in today's drill and practice programs. On the one hand, school systems do not have the material and human resources to develop effective software, they maintain; on the other, the private sector, with its press to produce programs for mass markets, will continue its "least common denominator" stance toward software.

In describing the low state of software development, critics pinpoint a major difficulty. However, the conditions they describe are not sufficiently compelling to justify the elimination of the instrumental approach to computer literacy. Information presented in this volume suggests that computer-assisted instruction, when compared to other approaches to the improvement of student learning, already offers one viable option to educators. Undoubtedly, future improvements in software will come slowly and incrementally, and the cost of hardware will diminish less rapidly than in the past; nevertheless, comparisons of CAI with competing strategies of instruction are likely to become more rather than less favourable over time. In the meantime, CAI provides students some computer skills and provides staff a stimulus and a medium for assessing traditional modes of instruction.

Literacy as algorithmic reasoning

Algorithmic reasoning, perhaps the most controversial concept of computer literacy, is a acquired through computer programming A.P. Ershov, a member of the USSR Academy of Science, has called programming the "second literacy". Literacy in reading and literacy in programming both have their origins in technologies- the printing press and the computer. Both support basic functions; "communications, work, the contemplation of nature and the struggle against it", and they "supplement each other, forming a new harmony of human mind".

Ershov suggests that the "acceptance of books blew up the integrity of word and action; it separated the process of knowledge accumulation from its application." Programming, with its emphasis on problem solving and on the clear comprehension of how to carry out what is to be done, helps rejoin, at least in certain types of tasks, what the book rent as under.

To become programmers, students must make effective use of algorithmic reasoning, Kemeny writes:

We have to learn to think in terms of algorithms, which are precise recipes foe solving problems or for accomplishing a task. A computer program describes an algorithm; it tells us "how to get there." Although algorithms were used and studied in mathematics in the past, there is today a strong prejudice in favour of formulae-that is, achieved results. But computers are forcing us all, even mathematicians, to readjust our thinking.

Algorithmic reasoning skills, Kemeny admits, are not easily articulated. Nevertheless, he suggests that programmers need to be able to express thought in very simple language (the small number of concepts available in a language like BASIC makes the task a demanding one); (b) to explain to the computer how to solve the problem (c) to divide complex tasks into small, clearly understood components; (d) to break down a procedure into simple steps and seek the logical relations among them; and (e) to find programming malfunctions and "debug" them.

While recognizing that programming can teach "procedural" thinking, Seymour Papert has stressed its potential for providing fundamental insights into mathematical and related abstractions. By using algorithmic reasoning to make the computer do their bidding, students can gain special insights into thinking and into the nature of knowledge. Put another way, learnings gained from programming can help students become their own "epistemologists".

Not only can programming develop generic reasoning skills, it can, its advocates contend, improve the quality of learning. Students, as programmers, are active and involved-preconditions for significant learning. Papert has also suggested that computers can bring constructive change to "sluggish and conservative" school systems. When teachers and students become skillful programmers, they move, he posits, beyond passive contexts to richer and more self-actualizing ones.

Some advocates of programming cast a critical eye on instrumental literacy because it places students in a passive role. As programmers, students can use computers in the active pursuit of their own learning objectives. If their responses are limited to those in programs developed by others, their imagination and learning are sharply constrained.

Papert and Kemeny, as advocates of programming, speak and write as trained mathematicians. Algorithmic reasoning an offspring of mathematics, can resolve precisely defined problems. It has repeatedly demonstrated its capacities to resolve technical problems associated with the development and use of microelectronic technologies. In fact, the expansive array of digital artifacts that lies at the heart of the computer culture is in one sense the product of algorithmic thinking.

However, the task teaching students computer programming differs markedly from that of teaching them to address effectively the human, social, occupational, and civic problems created by microelectronic technologies. These latter problems lie outside the rational world of computer programming and in the emotion-laden contexts of political organizations, work settings, family milieus, and other locales. Surrounded by keep conflicts, these formidably complex problems cannot be fully resolved through algorithmic reasoning.

The contentions that all students should acquire computer programming skills, then, should be viewed critically. To make computer programming a literacy standard for all students reflects a questionable strategy. Even if the standard is one which can feasibly be met by all students-a proposition that is far from self-evident-major investments in time and resources would be required to produce a narrowly based set of skills.

Literacy as education for altered roles

Noble has identified "consumer literacy". "worker literacy," and "citizen literacy" as the major role-related concepts. Although writers do not always define these terms in the same way, the concepts do accurately reflect prevailing views about which roles are being altered by computers and which ones can serve as foci for developing computer literacy.

Consumer literacy carries two meanings, one

linked more to hardware and the other more to software. The first stresses that individuals should be effective acquirers and users of computers and associated hardware. Since almost all families will eventually spend large sums of money on home computers and peripheral equipment, advocates of consumer literacy reason that schools should teach all individuals how to handle such expenditure wisely.

The second meaning of consumer literacy centres upon the "applications" individuals will be making "as part of their strategies for information retrieval, communication and problem solving". Advocates of this view optimistically project rapidly increasing flows of information out of, into, and through home computers. Individuals using the expanding sources of information will need requisite knowledge and skills. They will need to learn, for example, how to enhance their education through electronic media, exchange ideas through computer networks, and use shared databases to solve individual and community problems. Schools, then, should provide students with the literacy skills required to function in tomorrow's microelectronic environments.

Worker literacy is defined, on the one hand, as the skills needed to perform specific jobs and, on the other, as generic cognitive and information skills. The first definition presumes that the trend away from industrial jobs and toward information jobs will continue and, further, that career and vocational programs should teach individuals to perform such specific information jobs as computer repairing, systems design, and data processing. The second definition of literacy presumes that future job requirements will always be changing and that schools, more than ever before, should provide students basic skills which they can apply as their jobs undergo change or as they move into new ones. Workers in information-related jobs, in other words, need higher-level mental skills than industrial workers traditionally have had.

During the last decade, the impact of computer technologies on political environments is so far-reaching, some argue, that new approaches to citizen literacy are sorely needed. Today space and time no longer constitute barriers to national and international communication. However television and satellites are increasingly communicating political events through images, leaving it to citizens to search for the deeper political meanings behind appearances. Further, as the new technologies take over an ever-expanding number of government and business functions, they are posing far-reaching questions related to the privacy of individuals, equity of citizen access to the new media, and the role of computers in politics. All of these conditions, proponents of computer literacy argue, highlight the need for citizen literacy.

Actual descriptions of well-developed programs directed at consumer, worker, or citizen literacy are not as prevalent as are descriptions of other types of computer literacy programs. For one thing, they are more difficult to design and implement than are operational, instrumental, or algorithmic reasoning programs. Since the definitions of role-related needs are still ambiguous, organized content to support instruction is not yet widely or conveniently available. Finally, support for the idea that schools should provide students generic or higher-order learnings for use in consumer, worker, citizen, and other roles is growing.

Role-related literacy has not escaped criticism. Computer enthusiasts, some contend, have exaggerated the impact of the new technologies on job requirements, consumer demands, and citizen responsibilities. Levin and Rumberger, for example, suggest that the number of "information" workers required will be relatively small as compared to the number of janitors, cashiers, secretaries, and other service workers needed. Others contend that school and community leaders have launched literacy programs without adequate reflection. Some have blamed an "uncritical press" not only for exaggerating the need for literacy programs but also for providing "free advertising in the guise of objective reporting".

Many educators have tended to accept the claims of computer enthusiasts uncritically. Thus, criticism is needed to develop more realistic views about the educational significance of the new technologies. However, the claims of the critics can be accepted as uncritically as those of enthusiasts. Stated another way, criticisms that lack logical or evidential support need to be viewed skeptically. Critics of role-related literacy may be correct within an immediate time frame and incorrect within a longer-range time frame. Expanding computerization is changing consumer, worker, and citizen functions, even if slowly. Thus, today's critical messages about role-related literacy not only may prove to be errant; even worse, they may reinforce outmoded patterns and stifle the creation of needed new ones.

Advocates of computer literacy, then, have stimulated considerable thought about the concept during the last decade. Witness, for example, the analyses that increasingly dot the educational literature. By aggressively defining and diffusing multiple definitions of literacy and by skillfully linking them to diverse learning objectives, they have contributed significant;y to the development and diffusion of literacy programs. However, the mixed messages elicited by computers have slowed the diffusion of the concepts.

Literacy amidst a tide of clashing opinions

Some, seeing nothing new in computer technologies, indifferently dismiss them; in so doing, they rule out the "whither" question. Others, sensing a computer-created "revolution," urgently call for major adaptations in school programs and a through answer to the "whither" question. Given such disparate views, the first question facing those studying computer literacy is whether or not computer uses in schools indeed reflect another passing fad.

A passing fad or a continuing influence?

The indifferent, who "have seen it all before," believe firmly that the microcomputer is just another in a series of technologies without impact. They point to the high but disappointed hopes past educational leaders have had foe programmed texts, televisions, and related innovations. They conclude that after a period of uncritical use the microcomputer will have an uninfluential ending as have past instructional technologies. Since it is only one more in a long series, they ask why one should assume that it has more than passing significance.

The "passing fad" argument is erroneous because it is based upon a false assumption, namely, that the capacities and effects of microcomputers are similar to those of previous technologies. Microcomputers in fact differ substantially from past technologies. Because of their greater versatility and flexibility, they can be put to many more instructional uses. In additions, they can help manage instructional processes; versatilely access subject matter from libraries, information utilities, and other electronic sources; and facilitate the development of programs by students to meet their own objectives-feats that past technologies could not perform.

Computers differ from past technologies in a more fundamental way, namely, in their far-reaching effects on society. The impacts of programmed texts, for example, were confined to educational contexts. Even television, with its widespread influence, has not moved as deeply into society's institutions as has the computer. Microcomputers populate homes. work places, business enterprises, government agencies, social agencies, and other nonschool organizations. Having spawned a powerful array of novel industries, computers are now stimulating new dreams and aspirations, redefining human-machine relationships, shaping cognitive psychology, and altering modes of thinking. As computers change society, they create new educational needs, as already noted. Microelectronic technologies, then, represent much more than new educational means, they are surfacing profound questions about the ends of education. Therefore, they cannot be blithely dismissed.

The conclusion that the computer is not another passing fad does not imply that school purposes and programs will change rapidly. Powerful barriers constrain technological change. The new technologies do demand much more learning and change on the part of school personnel than have past technologies. The high costs of implementing literacy programs will slow diffusions processes. The clashing tides of positive and negative opinion, which surround decisions about computer uses, will complicate adoption decisions. Finally, it is significant that much larger private-sector investments are currently being directed at 'offices of the future' than at 'schools of the future', and 'at functions performed in business, military, telecommunication and government agencies in contrast to educational ones."

The new technologies have evoked both dark and bright scenarios. Optimists, emphasizing effective uses, see computers producing beneficial outcomes; pessimists, emphasizing misuses, see destructive and even dire consequences. While enthusiasts make expansive claims, skeptics decry these claims and cast them aside. Hope, optimism, and enthusiasm clash with fear, pessimism, and skepticism. The result is bifurcated views. That these views impinge directly upon the 'whither' question can be shown with some specific examples. The first set of examples is linked to current computer uses; the second, to presumed future impacts of computers.

Computer uses: beneficent or destructive?

Sherry Turkle has referred to the "Computer as Rorschach." The phrase is an apt one; computers do tap deep human emotions and elicit contrasting perceptions about their meaning and significance. Applications of computers in the political arena, for example, bring dissonant views. Some examples relevant to citizen literacy can help clarify the point.

Some have probed the impacts of the new technologies on individual liberty and privacy and have discovered an "electronic nightmare." Others, after studying national experiments in "teledemocracy," have concluded that the new technologies can help citizens influence public policy decisions. In a similar vien, some have observed that the power of "technological elites" constitutes a threat to democratic decision making; others see in the diffusion and use of microcomputers a new means. for advancing decentralized communication and democratic action. Or while some argue that linear thinking can be effectively applied to political problems, others contend that intuitive thinking will be required to solve these problems. Some believe that expanding international databases will enable leaders to address worldwide political problems more effectively; others contend that leaders from developing nations will suffer even greater inequalities in political opportunities because they will be unable to access the data. While the less sanguine stress that large technological systems, with "lives" of their own, cannot be controlled through political processes, the more cheerful contend that humans, as creators and users of these systems, can control their effects.

Contrasting positive and negative views, such as those just noted, have implications for research. Inquiry is needed to shed light on actual in contrast to presumed outcomes of computer uses. Some of the differences in view can be explained by the fact that scholars, in drawing their conclusions, use data about different but related phenomena as, for example, the computer's impact on a process (learning) in contrast to its impact on a value (privacy). However, a more fundamental problem is that the factual premises to support generalizations tend to be weak; effective research could uncover unreliable findings and false conclusions.

Perceptions about future consequences difer just as much as do those about immediate results. Thinkers often hold antithetical views, for example, about the long-range impacts of computers on the economic sector-views which have implications for "worker literacy" programs. Some, looking at the steady nfiltration of robots into industrial settings, conclude that the result will be a permanently unepmloyed "underclass"; others, examining the impacts of past technologies on unemployment, assert that the new technologies will create at least as many jobs as they eliminate. Some contend that the new machines will inevitably dehumanize work; others argue that comuters, by taking over the routine, will bring shorter work weeks and that this, in turn, will lead to more educational, social and other humanistic activities. While the optimists believe that ongoing research will make it possible for robots to perform increasingly "intelligent" functions, the least hopeful maintain that research break-throughs in artificial intelligence will be extremely limited.

The act that leaders and scholars hold such sharply divided views about the immediate and long-range significance of new technologies signals in still another way the powerful forces unleashed by computers. By surfacing conflictive and vital issues, the forces are stimulating and encouraging proactive thoughout. They also highlight the complexities policy makers face as they confront issues related to the "whither" question.

Whither computer literacy?

The pregious discussion has stressed that computer literacy is a young concept, that educational leaders have defined and implemented it in diverse ways, and that sharply clashing views surround its uses. At this point an important issue arises, namely, what framework can be used to analyze the newborn, diversely, interpreted, sharply contested and complicated concept of computer literacy? Since the history of the concept is short and relevant research is scarce, analogies offer one framework. Thus, acquiring computer literacy can be compared with the learning of a foreign language or the attainment of "book" literacy. Book literacy offers one fruitful analogy for probing the "whither" question.

Computer literacy and equal learning opportunity

Notably, book literacy and computer literacy are both similar and interdependent. The various symbols on the keyboard used to write this chapter are immediate indicators of the reciprocal relationships between written literacy and computer literacy. Other symbols, which appear from time to time on the screen. are additional reminders of the interdependencies between books and computers. These linkages underline a significant fact, namely, that individuals cannot acquire computer literacy without literacy in written language. Since one-fifth of the population of the United States is illiterate in written language, when more demanding measures are used, millions are locked out of computer literacy. The linkages between computers and books, then, suggest an important policy generalization, namely, that when school leaders make commitments to computer literacy they should not do so at the expense of traditional literacy programs.

Those comprising today's large illiterate populatin tend to be members of disadvantaged social, economic, racial and other groups. Since as a rule they have had limited access to written materials in their homes, they have long experienced unequal learning opportunities. Such inequalities, which still persist 500 years after the invention of the printing press, offer another lesson to those concerned with policy related to computer literacy. Unfortunately, the opportunities available to students pursuing computer literacy will undoubtedly be more inequitable, at least for the foreseeable future than will those available to students pursuing book literacy. Since computers and associated peripherals are much more expensive than books, educational agencies and parents will find it more difficult to provide children and youth the equipment needed to ensure equal opportunities. In addition, there are already public institutions that can diminish inequities in reading opportunities; however, public institutions to nurture computer literacy are not yet widespread.

If support for the concept of computer literacy continues, equlty issues will increasingly find their way onto the agenda of school boards. Some educational leaders are already addressing the issues. Affirmative programs directed at computer literacy during the summer, after-school scheduling to expand computer learning opportunities, and the use of such concepts as "student-access ratios" all reflect responses more random than widespread and more inchoate than well developed.

The Concept of "public information utilities" highlights the access question in the larger context of society. According enable all interested individuals to use large electronic databases to pursue educational, citizenship, and related purposes. Obviously, the implementation of this idea is at best a long-range possibility. It could not be realized untill more advanced technologies are achieved, new information norms and habits are developed, and the transmission of computer-based information becomes much less expensive nevertheless, the adjective "public" taht stands before "informatin utilities" denotes an already emergent sensitivity is society to the equity issue.

Given the very slow diffusion of reading skills during the last 500 yers, public funds to support electronic information excahnge will likely come slowly, if at all. The first to achieve new skills are usually not eager to transfer them to others. Thus, when individuals, centuries ago, acquired written language skills, they became members of an elite group; as elites, they opposed the broad sharing of literacy skills. For example, the reading elite in England in The nineteenth century "viciously criticized" the idea of free libraries for the common people. Arguing that such libraries would cater to the "popular passion for light reading-above all, for light fiction," the elite contended that the mass reading of such books would deter human progress, the common people would simply read the wrong things. It is possible that even today those who have acquired highly sophisticated computer skills tend to look down upon the use of games and drill and practice routines in schools.

Those opposing and those supporting the mass diffusion of literacy skills have confornted one another for centuries. Leaders on the side of the people, including the most disadvantaged, have prevailed, even though their struggle is not yet ended. Aided by powerful institutions, especially governmental agencies, they have repeated and acted upon a simple message, namely, that if individuals are to be enlightened and effective, they must be literate. If computers fulfill their educational promises, the struggle to eardicate inequitable learning opportunities will continue. As computer-utilities, and international promises, the struggle to eradicate inequitable learning opportunities will continue. As computer-driven interactive cable, electronic universities, information utilities, and international networks are increasingly used, equity issues will become more salient. Since microelectronic technologies are more complex, expensive, and mutable than books, the equity issues they raise will likely be even more difficult to resolve than those associated with written language.

The changing meaning of book and computer literacy

The five-century story about book literacy is broader than that of ever-expanding learning opportunities; it also encompasses a long struggle to define and redefine the goals of literacy in ways that reflect changing societal values. Thus, Patricia Graham, writing about literacy skills in the early 1980s, observed: "literacy... is what everyone needs in late twentieth-century America, both for their own good and for society's good." However, Horrace Mann argued, from a nineteenth-century perspective, that if students acquired literacy, vice would be reduced and morality would be improved- a view that in today's climate would strike many citizens as increadible. In mann's time, however, morality was such a salient value that school leaders coul not easily ignore it. Given the secularized public schools of today, Mann's definition of literacy is no longer highly relevant.

Definitions of computer literacy will probably follow in the footsteps of traditional literacy; they will, in other words, be temporary and impermanent. Rather than, policy makers will need to seek definitions and objectives that mesh with the needs of their time. Since the information society is much more mutable than previous societies, computer literacy objective will likely undergo more frequent changes. Given the many fearful messages about robots and related machines and their deep cultural roots, computer literacy decisions will also likely be more controversial. Witness, for example, the currency of the dark omens expressed a century and a half ago in Shelley's Frankenstein.

Given the long evolution of book literacy, what features best describe its patterns of growth?

For one thing, literacy definitions over time have become more complex—a pattern already reflected in computer literacy. For example, the simpler concepts of operational and instrumental literacy are associated more with the 1970s while the more complex concepts of computer programming and role-related literacy are linked more to the 1980s while the more complex concepts of computer programming and role-related literacy are linked more to the 1980s. The move from the uncomplicated to the more complex can be seen as follows: operational literacy requires minimal machine skills; instrunmental literacy requies minimal machine skills; instrumental literacy, the skills to learn from programs developed by others; algorithmic reasoning, the skills to create one's own programs; and role-related literacy, the skills to perform as competent consumers, workers, and citizens in the developing information society.

Given the pattern just noted, another question arises: What features best denote literacy's developing complexities? For one thing, more varieties of readint skill are now assembled under the literacy tent; for another, the functins served by literacy have multiplied.

Why are the meanings of literacy more encompassing today than they were earlier? Today's meanings stem from a multicentury trend toward an ever more varied content disseminated in a widening array of books, monographs, newspapers, magazines, and journals. When Martin Luther translated the Bible into the German language in the sixteenth century, he provided a powerful new stimulus and a popular means for the citizens of his natin to acquire literacy. At that time, however, literacy was by necessity defined largely in relation to one book. With the spread of the printing press and the growth and popularization of diverse types of knowledge, literacy expanded to include the skills needed to read more diverse matirals. In the nineteenth cntury, when individuals were pressed to understand the world around them by reading the newly invented newspaper, they had to expand their literacy skills.

As reading skills have expanded, literacy functions have become more differentiated. "Scientific", "mathematical," "esthetic," "technological," and "language" denote some of these literacy functions. They also symbolize bodies of knowledge that go substantially beyond those in Luther's day or, for that matter, in Horace Mann's time. Significantly, they imply high expectations for schools, and they help to explain the emergence of compulsory education.

Given continuing support of computer literacy. We can pridict that it will develop a pattern similar to that of book literacy; over time, its meanings will expand and become more differentiated. Although exact developments cannot now be foretold, it may be helpful to explore the "whither" question by Identifying smoe initial tendencies and by examining potential paths into the future.

Computer literacy has already undergone

considerable differentiation. Inherent in Previous descriptions of operational, instrumental, programmatic, and role-related concepts of literacy are such functions as word processing, computing, programming, information processing, and participation in teledemocratic arrangements. On the other hand, marvin and Winther, through a study of computer specialists, have arrived at a different set of functions. Employing an electronic mail questionnarie sent to users of the Advanced Research Projects Agency Network (ARPANET), a large computer network, they obtained perceptual data from respondents about "the major types of skills and levels of knowledte that organize comuper users into major classes." After analyzing their data, Marvin and winther posited five levels of users. These classes of users, along with pertinent functions and skills, are desvcribed here:

1. Many individuals each day come in contact with microwave ovens, candy machines, cash registers, and related devices; since they perform pasive rather than active functions, they do not require particular skills.

2. Members of the next group are called "tourists" or casual end-uers. Professors, who rely upon experts for data analysis, fall into this category. The skills "tourists" need are vey limited.

3. Programmers constitute the next group. They range from those who have wirtten one workable program to those who have wirtten model programs. The skills reqired buy

programmers, as already noted, are specialized ones.

4. Near the top of the hierarchy is the fourth group, called "hackers," who deal effectively with computer "logiams" and "bottlenecks." Their skills, which they express inventively, are highly technical.

5. At the top of the pyramid are "wizards." Noted for their capacity to perform "amazing feats," they can effect results seemingly by "passing their hands over circuit boards." Their skills are of the highest orger.

Marvin and Winther concluded that "the definition of literacy and its proper objects is at any time not only a standard of skillful performance but also a social sorting procedure for labeling certain tasks and domains of knowledge as worthy of social attention and effort." Thus, if computer users at IBM, the New York City public Schools, and the Pentagon had filled in the electronic questionnaire, their lists of functions and skills would likely have differed from one another and from those identified by ARPANET users. Given the diversity of their missions and "social sorting" procedures, they would, in other words, have arrived at different skills. Obviously, schools cannot prepare individuals to perform all computer functions; rather, they must concentrate on basic skills relevant to many differentiated functions.

Computer literacy- a provincial concept

If computer literacy skills are arrived at through

processes of social construction which go on in highly specialized organizations such as ARPANET, the following question becomes pertinent: How are current definitions of literacy, as described above, likely to be reconstructed in the decades ahead? the expanded and interrelated uses of microtechnologies provided one context for examining this question.

Since the microcomputer is the most visible of all microelectronic technologies, thinkers have understandably concentrated on computer literacy during the last decade. This approach to literacy has provided a useful focus for designing new learning experiences. However, "computer," as the modifier of literacy, may prove to be an impermanent concept. To be sure, microcomputers are pivotal points in the processing of information, however, they are only part of a much larger and more extended communication complex. The microcomputer is, to use concepts from gestalt psychology, a small "figure" against a more encompassing and expanding "ground."

While school leaders have been designing *computer* literacy programs, the french have coined the term "telematique". The concept, translated into English as "telematics," refers to the growing connections between and among computers and such telecommunication media as moderns, information utilities, microwave relays, satellites, and cable TV. As such, telematics reflects a new technological reality that transcends nations and cultures. Rooted in research and development breakthroughs, telematics carries special meanings. it draws attention to the unprecedented scope of current communication networks and to the invisibility of much of their operations. It highlights the connectedness of networks components and their collective and far-reaching potential for influencing local, national and global communication. Telematics, as a new symbol of the power of modern communication media, may well foreshadow the need for new literacy concepts. More specifically, children born in the mid-1980s, upon graduation from high school may find that computer literacy is a receding concept and that "telematic literacy" or some similar concept is making its way onto the educational stage.

Since the schools today are only beginning to link microcomputers to information utilities and thereby to provide students new sources of knowledge and ideas, the move away from computer literacy will surely be slow. However, even today we can see that the concept of *computer* literacy sharply constrains our perspective on the new technologies and on our capacities to comprehend their educational possibilities. since "computer literacy" misses many important meanings inherent in today's complex information environments, it is a provincial concept. If future citizens, workers, and thinkers are to come to grips with the needs created by the changing information society, today's ideas about literacy will needs to become more telematic. Such an expanded meaning will enable students to confront both the ends and the means of the microelectronic revolution. By using a telematic perspective, they can probe the promise of micro-technologies and contemplate the dangers that large-scale, rapidly proliferating and smoothly functioning telematic systems present to individuals and society.

The acceptance of a broadended concept of literacy will enable individuals to gain more than basic understandings of telematic systems and of their import for society. Given the remarkable progress already achieved in electronic information transmission, skilled individuals pursuing decision-making, work, educational, or other objectives can even today tap sources of information far beyond those immediately available in their homes and local libraries. Tens of thousands of adults are already accessing data through compuServe, The Source, and other information utilities; in addition, through electronic linkages, leading schools are providing some students with the skills needed to use these utilities.

As individuals learn to use electronic networks, they will be able to acquire information from new sources related to the solution of self-defined problems; to define, with the aid of other computer network members, technical and social problems and to seek solutions to these problems, and to develop with others new knowledge, products, and proposals. Form today's perspective such projections may seen unrealistic; however, when 1985 enrollees in kindergarten graduate from high school in the twenty-first century, they will step into a society where information is richer, more varied, and more accessible than it is today.

The power of computers and of their telematic companions to change society will surely have more far-reaching effects on the purposes of education than on the means of instructions since schools are now "in between" the descendant industrial and the ascendant information society, their purpose need to be reformulated. However, as Patricia Graham has observed, there is "much cacophony about practice" and "silence about purpose." In the decade ahead educational policy makers will likely be pressed to give more attention to the redefinition of purpose. such an emphasis will surface the educational needs the microelectronic revolution is creating. As new needs related to work, self-realization, citizenship, and other telematically influenced roles are identified, bases both for the updating educational purposes and for defining needed new book and computer literacy skills will be established.

Literacy as patterns of thought

Underlying the all significant concepts of literacy and educational purpose assumptions about desirable qualities of thought. Given the fact that the beliefs about desirable qualities differ, policy makers face a fundamental question: What types of thinking should the schools develop in students? Since the information industries have an insatiable appetite for newly created hardware and software products, their representatives tend to press for means-oriented thinking that can alleviate this appetite. Others, disturbed by the negative impacts of large-scale, computer-based systems on society, see the need for a different type of thinking.

The qualitative and quantitative needs for effective software systems in the future will grow markedly. Programmers responding to this need, as already noted, will apply algorithmic thinking, many other specialists engaged in the development and use of information technologies will be applying similar modes of "instrumental" thinking-modes that are notable for their technical problem-solving capacities, their highly rational expressions, and their effectiveness in dealing with means-oriented questions in here-and-now contexts. Proficient in procedural analysis, instrumental reasoning can add to an already astounding array of technical solutions and computer artifacts. Significantly, however, more and more critics argue that this type of reasoning cannot resolve the troublesome societal problems which microelectronic technologies are creating. Such reasoning, they contend, is too uncritical of the status quo, too constrained by machine requirements, and too blind and indifferent to the negative consequences of large-scale telematic systems to address overriding social problems.

Although critics have argued that instrumental reasoning lacks the capacities to deal effectively with a "permanent underclass," structural unemployment, the loss of privacy, clarification of purpose, inequity of access, nuclear warfare, and other problems created or exacerbated by modern technologies, they have not yet provided a clearly defined alternatives. Unless well-defined alternatives are developed, today's literacy programs, which are linked largely to traditional modes of thought, cannot easily be redirected. One place to look for the salient features of an alternative is in the computer culture itself. Outlined in broad strokes here are features of a type of thought nourished by the problems computerization is creating. Features dealt with include the scope of its perspective, its capacities for critique, the class of problems it addresses, and the outcomes it seeks. How the features depicted are related to the computer culture is also addressed.

The computer culture is encouraging thinkers to think more about the future than did members of previous cultures. Most of the history of book literacy transpired in rural contexts where tradition was a strong influence on thought. Since past patterns provided reliable standards for the future, rural thinking tended to be oriented toward the past. Those living in the dynamic computer culture, on the other hand, have found that past patterns are very reliable forecasters of emergent ones; consequently, individuals are pressed to anticipate and to think about the future in uncertain, rapidly changing, and sometimes threatening situations. Masuda has noted that the "purposeful use of future time" is a critical value of the information society. The founding in 1964 of the World Future Society, about the time the integrated circuit began to alter technology radically, is only one of many developments symbolizing the shift towards futures thinking. This thinking has found its way into thousands of publications in many languages; in addition, implementers of futures programs in schools are seeking to engender a type of thinking very different from that required to program computers.

Another concept of thinking spawned by the computer culture is associated with the term "global." Thinking directed at the development, programming, and operation of computers takes place in relatively bounded environments. As they pursue their objectives, developers are not pressed to probe the impact of their projected products on society, even though technologies have generated an array of complicated and largely unanticipated societal problems; paradoxically, at the same time technologies have eliminated barriers to worldwide, instantaneous communications and, in the process, have pushed global thinking to the fore. As a result, recognizing that sharply bounded definitions of problems suffer from missing ingredients, leaders are now applying the concept of "world problematique" to such disparate problems as energy and human equity. Expanding international databases are nurturing the budding trend toward global thinking. However, those engaged in such thinking face deeply conflicting national and world interests, as they think within almost unbounded perspective and as they strive to understand the intricacies of global issues.

Instrumental reasoning, by definition, is effective in the logical clarification of steps to be followed and procedures to be used in the attainment of specified objectives. Its mission is limited largely to the elucidation and implementation of efficient means. Users of instrumental reasoning tend to accept uncritically ends specified for them and to ignore the long-range consequences of the developments they achieve. Pursuing means in contexts where ends are determined by others, instrumental reasoners are not oriented toward larger issues of policy. This condition highlights another feature of needed thought, namely, a capacity to be critical about the ends sought in the information society and how these ends are related to the large-scale technological outcomes that instrumental reasoning help[s produce. This feature of thinking transcends narrowly proscribed contexts and concentrates upon purposive issues, strategic questions, and problems that center in public interests. Its target would not be the development and use of technology but the consequences of such development and use. Eschewing the procedural orientation of instrumentally oriented thinkers, it would be more intuitive and eclectic in its methods. Its bias would be toward holistic thinking and against narrower instrumental tendencies in thought.

To return to the "whither" question, even with its impressive accomplishments instrumental reasoning as a mode of thinking is an insufficient guide for those designing computer literacy programs. Thinking that would counter instrumental reasoning, as already implied, would be directed not at technologies but at the attainment of an effective society. Certainly, the ideal of self-realization of, in more specific terms, the fulfillment of the potential of individuals would become prominent in the design of computer literacy programs. To be sure, it is easier to develop machines than to nurture individuals and it is easier to generate information than to use it wisely. However, only developed individuals will be able to achieve an effective society and to fashion a positive story about life and achievements in the computer culture. Literacy programs directed at the self-realization of individuals in the unfolding computer culture will need a base in thinking that reaches beyond instrumental reasoning. Although the press for instrumental reasoning will continue in both society and schools, emergent signs suggest that a different type of thinking is now in the ascendancy-a thinking that is more futuristic, global, critical, holistic, and goal-oriented in its expression. Computer literacy programs based upon the emergency mode of thinking deserve priority; the complicity and the severity of the problems created by micro-electronic technologies require it.

Summary and conclusions

During the last decade, diverse meanings of computer literacy have emerged to guide program implementation. This chapter has highlighted four categories of literacy; operational, instrumental, algorithmic reasoning, and role-related. All categories include both skill and conceptual components. Algorithmic reasoning, for example, encompasses programming skills as well as high-order concepts while operational literacy includes introductory skills and simple concepts about computer components.

Programs based upon simpler concepts of literacy, while more widespread, are not as well integrated into curricula as are programs based upon more complex concepts. Activities directed at operational literacy, for example, are typically tangential to, if not outside, established courses; on the other hand, more complex concepts such as citizen literacy can be taught in existing courses. Since most literacy programs are not integrated into existing course. Since most literacy programs are not integrated into existing curricula, institutional support for them is likely to be weak.

Much controversy surrounds decisions about computer literacy. Computers, as increasingly powerful machines, activate deeply rooted cultural fears; changes now under way in human-machine relationships, the pessimists stress, will surely bring about a dehumanized society. On the other hand, computer also stimulate expansive new dreams for a more effective society in which humans, aided by machines, reach new levels of self-actualization. Leaders who address literacy decisions, then, are faced with two very different messages, one coloured by despair and the other by hope. These inharmonious views about the consequences of computers complicate literacy decisions.

Given the tender age of computer literacy concepts and the paucity of relevant research, the analogy of "book Literacy" can shed light on the query: Whither computer literacy? The history of book literacy contains clues about future developments in computer literacy. Thus, if computer literacy follows the pattern of book literacy, it will become increasingly complex, more expansive in its meanings, and more differentiated in the functions it denotes. Advocates of computer literacy will struggle long to realize equal educational opportunities as have advocates of book literacy; for several reasons, the former may face even greater challenges in attaining equity than have the latter. Paralleling the struggle to achieve equity will be another challenge, namely, that of ever redefining computer literacy objectives to make them consonant with changing standards of knowledge and with altered societal needs.

Since the computer is only a small figure in the larger context of electronic communication, it is already a provincial modifier of "literacy." A more fruitful and encompassing concept could be "telematic literacy", the latter provides a larger window foe viewing the understandings and skills needed to function in the developing information society.

All concepts of literacy contain underlying assumptions about what qualities of thinking schools need to develop in students. The press in the computer culture towards the development and use of hardware and software has required instrumental or means-oriented thinking. The limitations of this emphasis are becoming increasingly apparent; future concepts of computer literacy will need to place greater emphasis upon defining and implementing futuristic, global, intuitive, critical, ends-oriented, and holistic thinking.

2 Computers in Education

Invoivement in instructional computing in the School of Education, until the summer of 1979, can best the described as typical of other large universities. prior to 1979 most computing in education involved statistical work on a large mainframe computer or involved the requiring of computing background for these persons in a new select areas in education, typically prospective mathematics teachers or persons in academic programmes emphasizing statistical analyses of data for research purposses. For graduate students this involved batch processing of programmes for statictical, taken by most all graduate students both at the master's and doctoral levels. In addition doctoral research. At the undergraduate level only students preparing to be secondary mathematics teachers would have computing background. These students were required to complete at least one course in "computing," usually completed by taking the first course in Computing Science which includes programming in the pascal language, using batch and interactive processing on a large mainframe system. Many such students complete several courses in computing. The number of persons completing the secondary mathematics teacher certification programme has varied between five and ten per year, and has constituted about five per cent of undergraduates in both elementary and secondary teacher education. About 60 per cent of graduate students typically would make use of computers but this involvement was almost exclusively statistical analyses for class assignments and to a much lesser degree for research purposes. Less than 20 per cent of faculty were involved with computers for anything except statistical analyses for statistical analyses was not much greater than 20 per cent. The above figures are estimates, not precise calculations.

Attempting to incorporate a significant amount of computing in any coursework in the School of Education at this time required the use of batch processing on the mainframe system because of the limited availability of terminals. The only resident equipment within the School of Education was an ancient keypunch machine. The computing facility itself is approximately two miles distant.

The first attempt to break out of the mainframe "mindset" began with a request, in the Fall of 1971, for resident equipment for the school of Education. This followed by a few months the rekease by howlett-pacjard of their first "desk-top computer." These were labelled "calculators," a label which alleviated the problem of stisfying all the special rules associated with purchasing "computer". The single machine requested was to cost nearly $11,000. This first request was almost completely disregarded, since few educators felt there were any educational applications if these machine outside the areas if mathematics, science or statistics. Since the only possibility of use of existing computing facilities was batch processing or timeshare terminals on a large mainframe system and with little involvement in true instructional computing. The submission of requests for computing equipment for the School of Education was a twice yearly exercise which coincided with the cycle used by the university for equipment requests. Each request was slightly different from the one previous, reflecting progressive changes in technology. The physical size of the machines decreased the capabilities increased and costs dropped steadily. Each request was, for all practical purposes, disregarded.

This cycle continued until the fall of 1978 when an administrative change within the School coincided with the marketing of the first of the microcomputers. The first microcomputer for the School of Education was purchased in the summer of 1979. Some faculty feel that this machine was purchased mainly to see what would result as a consequence, with little expectation that it would have a significant impact. Since the receipt of this first microcomputer the School of Education at CU has seen considerable activity with respect to microcomputers and within the last year there are indicators of an acceleration of activity.

Current situation

In the three years since the first microcomputer arrived in the School of Education:

1. Twenty microcomputers are now housed in the School of Education. All of these machines are Apple II+machines with language cards. The decision to make all inital purchases Apple machines was based on at last two informal criteria. First, the primary focus of a school of education is education. It was felt that at the present time Apple machines have the greatest availability of educational software, and are the most common is schools. Secondly Apple machines were felt to be the most flexible. Therefore initial purchases, at least up to a number which could support standard university course instruction should be Apples. Once the minimal number of machines is reached then some purchases of other brands would be considered depending on their intended use.

   The most recent fifteen are housed in a "Microcomputer Laboratory". These fifteen machines are used in regular instruction in courses in the School of Education, laboratory work associated with these classes, courses in continuing education and "open" laboratory time for any interested user. The micro lab is housed in a room which is about 15m by 7m. The room has a chalkboard on one end wall and is equipped with electrical outlets on the remaining three walls in sufficient numbers and capacity to accommodate up to twenty-five stations. The existing fifteen stations arte situated so that when students are present they face the front of the room with the keyboards at their figertips. There are two chairs at each station allowing up to thirty students for a seheduled class. This arrangement appears to be the most beneficial for instruction given the equipment that is available. The lab is supervised by a student assistant during the open use hours. The specific schedule for use of the lab varies depending on the classes scheduled.

2. An NSF grant of $ 85,000 has been received tc conduct a project title "Personal computers abc Cross-Aged Instruction". This is a school-based experimental study utilizing nine complete microcomputer systems, seven of which have become the property of the cooperating school district, St. Vrain Valley Schools, and the remaining two systems are part of the permanent facilities of the School of Education.

There were four primary objectives of this project.

A. Increase the level of basic mathermatical skill of mathematically low-achieving sixth graders.

B. Increase the number of students enrolling in high school mathematics and science courses.

C. Evaulate the use of microcomputers as a unique instructional tool.

D. Develop effective applications of microcomputers in education.

These objectives were achieved by training high school students on the use of microcomputers and teaching then about the difficulties that sixth graders encounter in mathematics. Each of these studnets then tutored a sixth grade student every other school day for one semester. The project staff monitored both groups of students to determine the achievement of the objectives of the project. The experimental phase of the project was completed in May 1982. The interim report of this project is available through the ERIC system and the final report will be available in the spring of 1983.

3. The centre for management information technology in education has been formed to provide services to schol systems in the area of administrative uses of computers. Dr. James Rose is the director of this center. This center has provided on-site courses for school and school district administrators on the use of compouters in education administration, consulting services to schools and school districts and provided other support for schools and school districts in the area of the administrative use of information technology.

4. Several graduate courses have been instituted:

   A. "Computers in Education" is a survey course about computers and their use in education. The content of this course includes the history, characteristics, capabilities and terminology of computers: past, present and future of educational computing, both administrative and instructional; an orientation to microcomputer hardware and software; and includes on-site visits and demonstrations of current educational uses of computers. This course is designed for graduate students in all fields of education, is offered at least once per academic year and attracts theirty students per offering from many fields within ecucation as well as students from fields outside education. It is a popular course and provides the foundation for other courses in education computing as well as serving as a terminal course for those students wanting only an overview of the field. There are no prerequisites for this course.

B. "Computer Assisted Instruction" covers in detail the theory, design, development, implementation and evaluation of computer assisted instruction materials. Work on both mainframe and micro-computers is done in this course. Typically this course attracts students with some background in computing, some exposure to programming and some background in instructional design. This course is offered once per academic year and is designed for persons desiring in-depth work in the development of computer based instructional materials. It is anticipated that there will be increasing demand for this course.

C. "Microcomputers in the Classroom" is a hands-on course for educators wishing an overall orientation to microcomputers, their operation, software and rudimentary concepts of programming. This courses is offered three to four times per year including summer and attracts thirty students per section. Students from all areas in education as well as other disciplines are attracted to this course and about one half of the students are not degree candidates. The overall reaction to this course has been highly positive and it will likely remain popular for some time.

D. An undergraduate course somewhat parallel to the Microcomputers in the Classroom course described above has been scheduled for the fall semester 1982. This course will allow undergraduates to accumulate a greater amount of background on microcomputers than is included in the ten hours of instruction all such students will receive.

E. Other courses are planned for the future, some of which will be developed in the 1982-83 academic year. Areas to be covered in additional courses will be the more technical aspects of computers, authoring languages, programming and development.

5. The use of microcomputers is being incorporated into the graduate course in School Finance. Computers are used in this

course to model financial desicions and provide a base for projections for enrollments and finances within school districts. This course is taken primarily by persons seeking a school administration degree or certification and attracts about twenty-five students for each of one to two offerings per year.

6. Two sections of a semester long seminar on microcomputers for School of Education faculty and staff were conducted in the spring of 1982. This seminar dealt with the charcteristics, capabilities, operation, machine commands, software and uses of microcomputers in instruction and research in education.

The development and implementation of, and instruction in this seminar was the work of the writer of this paper. The seminar was not part of my regular assignment within the School of Education, but was done as a volunter effort on my part and followed by your weeks the delivery of the first five of the microcomputers for the lab mentioned above. It was arranged because of my personal commitment to the school and my sensing of the need and interest for such a programme for the faculty and staff of the School of Education. It was also my attempt to be consistent with advice that I give to school personnel when I am asked what they should do first twhen getting microecomputers in their schools. My recommendation under these circumstances is to spend a significant amount of time orienting their staff on the operation, use and potential of these machines, and to do this in a non-threatening supportive atmosphere. Only in this way will the staff support and envourage integration of micros into instruction.

Recruting for the seminar was accomplished merely by sending a memo to each of the faculty and staff of the school, asking who would be interested in a weekly seminar on the use and operation of microcomputers. Before the memo was sent it was expected that up to ten persons would reply. Theirty-nine persons indicated their interest and two sections were arrange at times which alowed the gretest number of participants. Only one person could not attend one of the two sections. The level of interest can be ascribed to three things. First is the visibility that microcomputers had received in education in the recent past. Second was the general knowledge that the faculty had of my activities with respect to micro-computers over the previous two years, and third was the positive relationship I have with most all the faculty.

The seminar met once per week for a full semester each session lasting two hours. The content of the seminar included an overview of features and capabilities of micro-computers, rudimentary concepts of machine control through machine commands and programming in BASIC; demonstrations of word processing/text editing, data management software and spread sheert software; a demonstration of LOGO; and demonstrations of commercial instructional software including drill and practice, toturials, simulations and games. There were numerous handouts given in the seminar, all locally prepared and there were few demands made on the participants for outside work. Most all outside work was self-imposed by those participants who found the time, had sufficient interest and felt the need to have additional work on the machines. Five machines were available at almost anytime a participant desired to have machine time for "outside work."

The primary desired outcomes for the seminar were machine familiarization, getting the concept of machine control through machine commands and programming, overcoming machine anxiety, exposure to the more common types of software and to foster a positive attitude toward this new technology and its use in education.

Since the completion of the seminar several faculty have become involved with microcomputers who were not involved previously. The general reaction to the seminar was highly positive based on a written evaluation. No tests, quizes or term papers were required partially because the participants and I were all colleagues and friends and partially to maintain a relaxed atmosphere. All feedback thus far has been positive and the apparent general feeling is that the individual objectives of the participants were achieved. Even the instructor is positive.

7. Several in-service courses for both teachers, administrators and others have taken place. In the past one and one-half years nearly ten

courses relating to micro-computers have been conducted by faculty in the school or with the equipment in the school. These have been primarily orientation courses for school administratiors and teachers. The content of these courses varies with the intended audience and with the specifics of the request for such a course, or; something similar to the content of the faculty seminar is common except the depth of coverage depends on the amount of time available. The course credit has varied from zero to three semester hours and the courses have taken place both in the School of Education and in schools around Colorado, with participants providing their own equipment when the course is off-campus. Requests for courses in this area typically address the need to upgrade the background of school personnel in an area where little backgound exists. It is anticipated that this need on the part of school personnel will be present foe osme time and more such sessions are expected. Coursework beyond first courses such as these are typically satisfied through regular course offerings or specially designed courses in response to specific requests. Such coursework may or may not fit into a degree programme.

8. A School of Education committee for the corodination of efforts in education computing within the school has been formed. This committee is a Dean's committee and consists of the five persons most directly involved in

using computer technology in the School of Education. The committee addresses questions relating to the priorities on the use of and acquisition of equipment, advises the dean on policy decisions related to computers in the School of Education, oversees possible duplication of effort among existing and proposed courses involving computing and co-ordinates efforts for the entire School on matters involving computers. The committee was established by the dean as an alternative to the more traditional approach to the apperance of a new area which is to create a new programme of division. It was felt that a committee would allow more flexibility at least in the initial stages of activity, seemed to be the more appropriate arrangement in an area which is more inter-discipinary than existing areas in education and better accommodates the rapidly changing nature of the field.

The future

Because of the rapid changes that are taking place in computing in general and in educational computing and due to the increasing demand for courses and programmers in this area several activities and events will take place in the near future in the School of Education. The faculties in elementary and secondary education both have approved the incorporation of a programme for an orientation to microcomputers in education for all undergraudate teacher educate students at the University. This programme is to commence in the fall of 1982 and will include approximately ten hours of instruction. The specifices of the content and scheduling of this programme are not yet firm., but will most likely include an overview of computers and their use in instruction, technology, features of hardware, machine operation and demonstrations of instructional software.

2. Within existing graduate degrees emphases in several areas related to educational computing are being considered. One emphasis is for those persons wishing to concentrate on instructional systems and computers. Many of these persons will likely find employment in educational settings in industry. A second emphasis would be for persons planning to remain in school classrooms but wish concentrated work on instructional computing. A third emphasis would be for persons wishing to purse supervisory positions in instructional computing in school systems. Each of these emphases has somewhat unique needs for graduate work. Each of these emphasis could make use of coursework in computer science in addition to the coursework in education. Coursework in computer science is available since their are existing graduate degrees in computer science on campus and two new undergraduate programmes in computing are being implemented on campus, one in computer science-engineering and another in the College of Arts and Sciences. The possibility of interested persons choosing one

of these new emphases and the availability of supporting coursework in computer science will provide competent persons for positions in schools, school systems and industrial training.

3. The dean's committee will be addressing several questions of logistics and questions of future equipment needs and priorities. Logistical questions include the scheduling of laboratory time, instructional time and resulting machine use; financing expendable materials associated with the laboratory; the availability of materials and how to address increased faculty use in light of increased use instruction and by others. An important question that must be addressed concerns future purchases of equipment and what kind of equipment should be purchased. Up to now all purchases were Apple machines, for the reasons cited above. It is anticipated that deviation from this will likely take place in the near future since we are approaching the minimally adequate number of Apple machines for regular instruction. Pressure is already being felt to begin looking at other machines for various uses other than direct instruction.

4. Interative video equipment has just newly arrived. Involvement in this field will begin soon but the direction to be taken in this area has yet to be decided. The use of interactive video may prove to be an area of application of computer technology as exciting for

education as many say the microcomputer will be.

It is clear that the activities which have taken place in the past three years are the predecessors of many more activities in the future. These activities will involve many more persons, than before as more faculty become comfortable with the equipment. It is anticipated that this activity will accelerate, due in part to the faculty seminar and the increasing availability of equipment. This will necessitate greater co-ordination to minimize the duplication of activities.

Without a broad base of faculty support and familiarity with the field little integration of educational computing into the programmes of the School of Education can be expected. Thus the philosophy to date has been to direct initial efforts for the incorporating microcomputers into the School of Education by the orientation of faculty and staff. We have succeeded in this thus far, however this has not been to the exclusion of other efforts, as can be seen by the above list of activities over the past three years. Increasing availability of equipment has allowed greater numbers of persons to become involved. with additional changes in technology, questions concerning the direction to be taken in the future will have to be addressed. Weighing these needs against a myriad of other demands on finances and personnel is a difficult process.

The School of Education of the University of colorado-Boulder is in much the same position as schools elsewhere. We do feel, however, that we are ahead of others in getting the total faculty and staff involved. The nearly eighty per cent participation in the faculty seminar will and has caused faculty who would otherwise not be involved to develop creative ùses of these machines. In other ways we are experiencing the same technological growing pains that others experience. We are fortunate to have a supportive administration at both the School and University levels. The question of what to do for the pre-service teacher education students is being addressed and action will be taken soon. We force' that the next few years in education will be challenging and exciting because of the pressure of technological change. We see greatly increased activity in computing in education and plan to be leaders in this field.

Computing and education at teachers college

This paper disrobes the computing and educational activities at Teachers College, Columbia University, in mid-19832. All the activities presuppose certain ideas and beliefs about computing, so these are outlined first. Individual activities and their mixture have been shaped by the tradition of Teachers College, so that tradition is briefly summarized next. Several illustrative activities are presented next, each in a separate, descriptively subtitled section of its own. The staff responsible for those activities and the facilities used are summarized next. The paper concludes with a look ahead.

Presuppositions about computing education

Computing will expand the focus of educators to include for more attention to process. Though end products such as the problem's solution or the finished essay will remain important, computing will sharpen attention usefully upon how such products are produced, helping the learner to become more self-sufficient by helping her or him to understand and improve the process that creates the products.

Computing will raise graphics to a new level of importance, particularly when compared to text. Dynamic images and means to create, store and manipulate them will become as commonplace to future learners as parallel activities with text have been to preceding generations.

Computing will so permeate out lives that broad computing literacy will be absolutely essential. Those in education must help to develop that literacy, across the entire population.

Computing will permeate and inform the entire curriculum, even as theology did in medieval universities. It will no longer be seen as something for mathematicians only but will be used integrally from one end of the curriculum to the other, even by people who see themselves as "non-scientific" or "non-mathematical".

Computing will be used in many different modes within education, and none of these modes should be neglected by those seeking to improve education. Though "tutee" or discovery/exploration computing may be exciting and fulfilling in the right situation, excellent tutorial software will always have available role to fulfil, as will other more tightly constrained software systems.

Programming and being able to programme in several languages will remain a valuable background of anyone wishing to play a key role in the application of computing within education. Knowing what lies behind either a successful piece of software is critical in imagining the next step.

Evaluating and developing software are both essential skills for any one seriously applying computing to education. Extensive practice with each is indispensable.

Broader human issues, the self-proclaimed expert in computing and education and the vendor have no interest in nor time for, must be constantly considered and debated. Institutions with some mass must be among those who continually press ahead with examining such issues.

Technology needs imagination, and educational computing needs it as desperately as any technological activity we have ever engaged in. literature, drama, art, music and other traditional activities must be continually re-experienced by those designing computers and computing software for education so that our technological creations stretch the mind rather than shrink it.

Teachers college, Columbia University

Teachers College is the graduate school of

education associated with Columbia University. It enrolls more than 4000 students across three major divisions focusing respectively upon psychology, health and nursing, and instructional institutions and programmes. The activities of computing and education are housed within the division of instruction, a division which also houses the traditional instructional areas such as math education, science education, and music and art education, as well as such newer areas as TESOL and bilingual education. There are between forty and fifty students enrolled for degrees specifically in computing, mostly at the masters level. Undergraduate and graduate students in computer science are in a completely different part of the university and utilize separate computing facilities from to se mentioned below as belonging to Teachers College.

During its near century of existence, Teachers College has had a major influence on education, both in this country and around the world. If there is one thing that characterizes that influence more than anything else, it is its breadth. unlike other major private schools of education,Teachers College has tended to aim its programmes, courses, and public proclamations at the mass of educators rather than the academically elite.

In computing, this is reflected in our attention to literacy, to broad programming skills, to a masters level programme aimed at those without computer scientific skill, and to an attempt to develop materials and books that will be useful in educating a wide range of educators. It is also reflected in our attempts to incorporate computing into the entire curriculum, both in field projects and at the College itself. We believe the development of highly technical skills is best left to computer science colleagues; our job is to encourage them in the right directions, to creatively apply what they develop to education, and to make the mass of educators aware of the implications of the results.

As the College reaches its centenary, computing will be an increasingly integral part of all its academic activities. The concomitant transformation in what instruction means and how it is best carried on should be visible and intelligible to the average educator around the world.

Computing and education ectivities

Programme/Department

In 1975 a modest masters degree programme in computing and education was established at Teachers College. In 1981, it was merged with two older programmes. Communications and Instructional Technology, to form the new Department of Communication, Computing, and Technology in Education.

The new department was formed because faculty and students in the three programmes shared so many concerns and interest. They include, the effects of electronic mediation upon communication, the impact upon human communication of dynamic computer graphics, the meaning of the non-verbal formss of some computer activities such as arcade game playing, the implications for education of what MacCluhan dubbed the electronic "global village", and the relation between traditional skills in instructional design and programmed instruction and the development of computer-based software.

Degree

Since 1975, the college has offered a popular masters degree in computing and education. It requires about 10 courses, five which must be from those listed in the section below subtitled Courses, and two which in turn must be Programming I and II. Apart from Programming I and II, the course selected by and approved for the student depend significantly on her or his undergraduate major, work experience, and career interests. A course usually meets an hour and forty minutes, once a week, for a term. In this programme, it usually involves work on several computers, outside lass, either independently or with partners in a lab. Most students are employed full-time somewhere in the New York metropolitan area, so all courses are scheduled in the evenings or o Saturday. The typical load is two courses per term, so it usually takes two years to complete a masters degree.

In the new department, students may also pursue a doctorate in either communication or technology, with a major in computing. In such programmes, students must complete 90 points and a dissertation.

Though tailored to the individual, each

doctoral student's programme would normally include most of the 10 course listed below, several courses from communication and technology, courses on test construction and curriculum development psychology and other relevant areas, and from 10 to 20 points of independent study focussed on the dissertation. As with other Ed.D. programmes at Teachers College, up to 45 points can be granted for comparable level work done at author institutions, provided the advisor approves it as relevant.

The dissertation need not be primarily a document like a Ph.D. thesis; it can be software or other comouter related materials, accompanied by a relevant justification and appropriate documentation. We expect, for example, that the new course in software development will naturally lead to dissertations for some students.

Students are also expected to intern and assist, either in the Microcomputer Resource Center, in courses, in various field projects, or in combination of several of these activities.

Courses

The following are the ten computing courses now being offered in the department. The many offerings focussed more specifically on communication or instructional design are not shown, nor are seminars, colloquia, and internships common to the entire department.

Computing Literacy

An overview of computers within society,

particularly education. Demonstrates, readings, and hands-on participation introduce a wide range of computer applications and underlying concepts. Assumes no computing experience.

Programming

Communicating with computers and humans through programmes. Uses FPL, a new language designed to clearly introduce fundamental programming concepts, and either BASIC or PASCAL or both. For beginners or experienced programmers.

Computers and Writing

The use of computer text editing and processing systems in writing. Focuses on writing as a process, synthesizing psychological theory about writing with current computer capabilities. Assumes no computing experience.

Computers and the language arts

Demonstrations, theoretical review and practical work with software for teaching reading, writing, grammar, and literature in English and other languages. Assumes no computing experience.

The computer as an instructional aid

A range of computers are used to explore specinc commercially available products and services that apply computing to instruction. Computer as tutor, tool, and tutee

Programming II

Prerequisite: Programming I. Extension of Programming I. Applies programming to significant problems through team programming projects.

Teaching computing

Prerequisite: Programming II. Explores and practices pedegogically sound ways to teach computing and especially programming to a range of students, including those outside math and science. Includes limited teaching activities.

Computer graphics

Prerequisite: Computing literacy, Programming I, or comparable introduction. Introduces basic types and applications of computer graphics, particularly but not exclusively in education. Explores various hardware and software systems, provides some hands-on experience, but not programming.

Software evaluation

Permission required. Introduces a range of evaluative instruments and techniques and applies them, through student teams, to a number of representative, commercially-available instructional software programmes and packages.

Software development

Permission required. Team approach to developing computer-based educational software in a variety of academic subjects. Complete modules and systems of software will be designed, programmed, tested and documented.

Developing methods and materials

Since a major problem in integrating computer education into teacher training is the lack of models to emulate, methods to adopt, and materials to utilize, we have tried to make our work serve not only or immediate Programme needs but also the needs of other schools and departments of education as well. That is, we have tried to create materials that embody our developing methods and models, so that others may begin with more than we did.

The programme in computing and education and the various courses are models that embody methods which can easily be copied or adapted by the many students who graduate. Certainly they will make use of some or all of them, thus avoiding some of the initial efforts we had to make. But those who never study here will not benefit very directly from such adoption. We therefore have published some of our materials so that a wider audience may profit from them. Two examples will illustrate.

FPL: A Language for learning programming. The language we use to teach teachers programming is FPL. The language and the material reflect our assumption that most people will learn more than one language, and that the first one learned should be well structured, graphic, and simple. Accordingly, FPL is taught first but is linked to the learning of both BASIC and PASCAL, in such a way that even the Basic programmes developed are well-structured and easy to read and maintain. FPL is simple, including only one graphic ikon or image for each of the foundation elements of classical programming. The language is presented as we use it in Programming I and II, including our work in both BASIC and PASCAL, in the text *Programming Primer*

We have also developed a tutorial interpreter for FPL which greatly speeds of the learning of syntactic and definitional details of the language. Both book and interpreter assume that learning occurs most consistently from copying and modifying models and that the best materials take seriously the learner's point of view, providing help and explanation in enough detail to be useful to the novice, but in a form and location where they can be conveniently skipped over by the learner who does not need them. Though only available under test status now, the interpreter will be made publically available on several types of machines in due course.

Tutor, tool, tutee: A Framework for grasping diversity. To bring teachers more rapidly up to a position where they can wrestle with th educational implications of widespread integration of computing into education, we encourage them to use topologies, analogies, and other classificatory frameworks to categorize diverse examples of computer use in education.

Such an example is used in *The Computer in the School.* That book represents the whole field of computing and education by a collection of nineteen pioneering articles, and suggests a three category framework to simplify coming to terms with that diverse field.

By presenting several quite different types of educational computing and their implied presuppositions, this material make it difficult for a student to easily maintain too narrow a perspective on what educational computing is. Act the same time, by the presentation of an appropriate framework, such material enables the students to superimpose enough order on the diversity to remain comfortable with its very breadth. Thus the learner can immediately assume a realistically broad outlook without feeling lost in the chaos.

Special conferences

Since by their general design, association conference leave many relevant topics either totally unexplored or barely examined, we also sponsor specially focussed conferences from time to time. We hope these conferences, when they are any good, will also serve as models.

The conference on Child Appropriate Computing which we held in 1981 is a good example. It was designed to make vendor products the focus of conferee evaluation and thus to determine the extent to which hardware and software marketed as appropriate for children was actually appropriate or inappropriate for them. Ten vendors or developers came in and the one hundred conferees were divided into ten teams of ten members each. Each team spent one day evaluating four of the products, each in a one hour session. Each vendor made an identical presentation four times during the day, to four different teams. The presentation could take any forms the vendor or developer thought would best show off his or her products' child appropriateness. The evaluations were then written and pooled, and a closing discussion was held in which the evaluations and their import were summarized. By focussing on this topic and upon selected products, conferees and vendors alike got a deeper perspective on what was and what was not child appropriate about the products presented.

Software evaluation

A good bit of effort goes into systematic evaluation of instructional software at Teachers College. A funded project involving several micros and hindreds of hours of graduate student time continues to examine software and refine instruments and techniques for evaluating it. The EPIE project regularly publiches its findings through channels it earlier established for disseminating reviews of text books and other non-computer-based instructional materials. The knowledge of the evaluators and the presence of the software are rich sources of information and material for staff and students in the programme, not merely those few actually doing the EPIE evaluations.

Research

At Teachers College, both inside and outside the department principally concerned with computing, considerable research dealing with computing and education is in process. Some concerns how adults learn programming, some how children learn both programming concepts and other ideas related to using computers, some what teachers need to know beyond a language such as LOGO if they are to use it effectively in a normal classroom, and so on. By far the most extended research activity in computing and education here now, though concerns the use of computing in writing. Under several separate grants, we have been both developing a more appropriate text editor/writing prompter for children and studying how the use of computers in writing affects the quantity and quality of their writing. We believe that a major impact of computing in schools will be improve the learning of writing, and hope our work will provide useful materials in their are, too.

Other departments at Teachers College are also beginning to conduct research into various aspects of using computers in education and that work can only be expected to increase in the immediate future.

Field work

At this time considerable assistance is being given to a number of school districts, primarily in terms of short term training delivered by graduate students, going out to the districts requesting such help. The scope of this work varies widely, from one visit to arrangements that span several years. The latter kind are the most useful in terms of providing more solid help to the districts and some steady income to graduate students. Some of this work has been written up but most has not. We regard it as important not only for the help it offers districts but also for the research opportunities it may afford. unfortunately, though some of our graduates are setting themselves up to do this sort of in-district training, there remains a shortage of people really qualified to do it here, just as in the rest of the country. Qualified people can make so much more money by applying their computing skills elsewhere, that few find this sort of work attractive for long.

Facilities and staff

Facilities

The computing activities here utilize the DEC 20/60, the various micros in the Microcomputer Resource Center, and indirectly, the many micros people now have access to at home or at work.

Central time—sharing computer Approximately 20 of the erminals directly connected to the DEC 20/60 are available 24 hours a day, seven days a week on a first-come, first-serve basis to the several hundred students in various departments who make some consistent use of the computer. An additional 20 phone lines are also available, on the same terms, to those having access to a suitable, dialup terminal. In addition to FPL, BASIC, and PASCAL, several editors and a great variety of other software are availabole to students uing this central time sharing system. Students in the programme must use this system for some of their work evenif they do most on one or more micros. We believe students should be familiar with both large and small systems.

Microcomputer resource center. The MRC includes both micros and helpful humans and togethe they play an important role in many of our activities. There are currently about 20 machines there of 6 different types and a vast array of instructional software. The staff include a director and 5 to 10 graduate students, each of whom puts in a few hours a week. Some staff double as instructors in orientation and training scheduled for the MRC; some double as software evaluators in the on-going EPIE software evaluation project. Most are familiar with several micros and a variety of software and thus can be usefully informative to students an teachers visiting the MRC.

Other facilities. because they are establish in jobs, and increasing number of our students have access to one or more computers either at home, or at work, or both. We encourage them to use these computers if at all possible, both to lessen the load on our own facilities and to tie the computing of such students more closely to machines they will primarily use outside Teachers College. Because of the range of research going on, there are also a number of micros available on a more limited basis, to selected students, usually those connected with the research project to which the micro belongs. There are about 10 machines in this category now, mostly Apple II's.

Staff

The departments has four professors, one of whom does nothing but computing and education, one of whom splins between instructional design and computing, one of whom spends a minor part of his time on computing, and one of whom spends full time in other areas of the department. In addition, the department has a full time instructor in computing and a number of part-time instructors who teach or assist with one course. There are two faculty members elsewhere in Teachers College who also spend most of their time on computing and education, one on the psychological implications of that computing, the other on administrative and management aspects of computing in schools nd colleges. The department has a number of other adjuncts and instructors who are quite active in computing, typical examples being one in computing and writing and one software evaluation.

Future directions

At this time, we see the future only dimly and only the near future at that. So far as Teachers College is concerned, we think hat eventually courses in computing and history, computing and music, and so on will spring up and become part of the curriculum in each separate subject area, so they will not be housed except temporarily in the department or programme of computing. At the same time, we think most schools and departments of education and teacher training will have separate programmes or sub-departments specializing in computing in education. While it may be true that computing should be integrated into other subjects, computing is and will continue to be a subject in its own right as well. It has emerged as a politically separate entity within the university curriculum and is emerging as a separate entity in the school curriculum as well, particularly in the form of courses on programming.

We think the implications of extensive computer usage in schools will be an important focus of study for some time to come, particularly in terms of graphics, interactivity, modelling, process, and problem solving. As the routine aspects of computing in adduction become normal parts of the traditional methods courses and as people arrive already knowing how to programme as well as in necessary, our attention will increasingly be focused on what it all means. It many be that along with introducing artificial intelligence to schools, we may increase artificial ignorance. If some, we will have lots to think about.

Teacher education curriculum for the 80's

Recall "The Saber Tooth Curriculum"- a satire on education, authored by Peddiwell with a foreword by Harold-Benjamin? This curriculum taught the students the fundamental of fish-grabbing-with-bare-hands and Saber-tooth-tiger-scaring-with-fire even after the tigers disappeared and fish nets were invented. Are, we, in teacher training, caught up in supporting a curriculum which has been effective during the past five years but which may be totally inappropriate for the next five?

The other day two professors from a school of engineering were discussing the merits of certain programmes within their department On professor felt that the school's obligation was to put an engineer into the field who could function with the existing technology. The other professor felt that, since the technology would change before the student graduated, it didn't really matter what the student was taught as long as he/she possessed necessary learning skills. Five years hence, the student would still be an engineer only if he or she could keep up with fast changing developments in the field. To a certain degree, we who are in the profession of training classroom teachers are faced with a similar task.

It is clear that the computer will have a dramatic impact on the classroom during the 80's. A current survey conducted the Oregon Department of Education has revealed that over 50 per cent of Oregon's schools are now using computers for instruction. Minnesota alone has 20,000 microcomputers in 1800 secondary and elementary public schools. The state of Alaska has adopted telecomputing as an integral part of their statewide educational system. Alaskan school systems consider the microcomputer a standard instructional tool and teachers have readily accepted its presence. Pitka's Point, a remote rural school districts of 37 students provides eight APPLE microcomputers for general instructional use. Anchorage, the largest district in the state, has well defined and articulated computer curriculum serving all 73 schools with computer-assisted learning. From Alaska to Florida, schools are budgeting for microcomputer equipment and supplies. By 1984, is is expected that over one million microcomputers will have found their way into the nation's schools.

Today's freshman is tomorrow's beginning teacher. how can we prepare this teacher to cope with the existing technology and yet be equipped to face the demands of tomorrow's classroom? We have entered an era which will be known as the Communications Revolution. We must give the teacher entering this transition period the skills needed to survive the entering this transition period the skills needed to survive the first few years in the traditional classroom and yet build a foundation of knowledge needed to cope with the developing technology.

Tomorrow's teacher must be an effective manager of learning rather than the principal source of knowledge. In tomorrow's classroom, through the use of telecommunications, the student will be able to call up information on almost any subject. Many of the files accessible to the student could be learning episodes on various topics. Accessibility to information will not be a problem, but for learning to take place, some structure needs to be imposed on the sequence of accessing this information. The computer can keep records on students' interaction with episodes, but the teacher needs to interpret the record's meaning. It will be the teacher's responsibility to work with the student and the information system to help the student, maintain a reasonable learning pace. More of the teacher's time in the future will be taken up with the task involved in assessing, diagnosing, prescribing, directing, and managing the instructional process. Ways will have to found to help teachers manage the instructional environment more effectively if there is going to be time for the teacher to interact with student's.

The microcomputer presents the teacher with the opportunity to individualize instruction. No matter what delivery systems are created, there are certain aspects of learning which must be considered. Living in a society where we are interdependent, students will still need to gather together to foster social interactions and to learn how to live in a supporting manner. An educational environment will have to exist that will allow students to learn how to acquire and process information. Some areas such as mathematics, language, arts and reading can be assimilated at the student's learning pace independent of the state of the group to which they are attached.

What kind of skills must our teachers posses? Every teacher, in addition to having a basic subject matter competency, must be aware of subject matter resources and be trained in their evaluation. Every teacher must have some management training in order to effectively monitor students learning. The teacher must be able to organize and direct group activities. Finally, in order for the teacher to encourage students to progress on and independent basis, he/she must master the available technology to support the learning environments determined by student needs.

To meet these needs, the pre-service and in-service training must:

1. Educate teachers to be managers of information.

2. Prepare teachers to be leaders of group process.
3. Train teachers to diagnose and place students within a learning system in which the student can make progress.
4. Instruct teachers to operate the equipment that will be used to help deliver the content.

All learning environments that permit student advancement on an independent basis require elaborate record keeping systems for tracking student's progress. Most future systems will be computer controlled so that record keeping does not impede a student's movement toward a defined goal. Within the next ten years students will no longer be dependent upon the teacher to begin a lesson. Students will be able to engage in a dialogue with the computer which will help them advance in fundamental skill development at a rate that is not possible within today's classroom. The teacher should understand the technology of such systems in order to maximize his/her effectiveness. How should the teacher training curriculum reflect the needs of this learning manager? Future teachers need to be involved with computer based education throughout their college experience. Appropriate preparation includes a lower division computer literacy course and series of involvements with the microcomputers within other courses.

The student is required to demonstrate an ability to interact with microcomputers and run application software. The student is expected to explore the impact of the computer on society. The student is required to write reports on the above activities and is expected to use the microcomputers as a tool to accomplish this task.

The computer should be used as a learning tool within the student's college classes. Students need to experience how one learn via the computer. At WOSC we are in our third year of a National Science Foundation-Comprehensive Assistance to Undergraduate Science Education grant titled "Infusion of Computer Science into Liberal Arts and teacher faculty member per year concerning the potential of the computer as an educational tool. This is accomplished through a two week summer workshop during which time the faculty member defines a project to be implemented doing the course of the following year with grant support. Through these activities we have begun to incorporate the computer as a teaching tool in several courses in various departments on campus. The most successful applications to-date have been in the Music, Dance, English Composition, Biology, Mathematics, Education, and Psychology areas.

First year CAUSE projects

Special Education/Psychology-computer-aided testing, software programmes for lab experiences, and student scoring of their own personality inventories.

Music—pitch and interval ear raining and multi-voice score training.

Physics—wave motion demonstration programme.

Mathematics—Intermediate Algebra competencies and data research on testing.

Chemistry—organic compounds nomenclature practice.

English—composition editing using word processing.

Education-application of on-line computer-administered testing.

Second year CAUSE projects

Psychology/Special Education-statistical teaching packaged.

Economics/Business -record keeping system, simulations of running a profitable business, and fiscal management.

Biology-use of pre-packaged programmes in General Biology and demonstration of various programmes to elementary teachers.

Mathematics- graphing programmes for trigonometry and vocabulary.

Education -collection and analysis of student data and transfer of that data to a statistical package.

For the education majors, additional training is required to lay the foundation for using computers as an instructional tool.

Very few instructors write primary textbook materials, yet almost all instructors create supplementary materials. Similarly, the typical classroom instructor will not be writing computer programmes, but will be creating or managing supplementary materials.

The focus is on helping the instructors learn to choose and use good application software in their classroom and to use the computer as a management tool. The following topics are covered in the foundation block for elementary and secondary educational:

1. Computer managed records

(a) Grade book

(b) Test banks of questions

(c) Achievement records

2. Drill and practice material

3. Tutorials

4. Entire curriculum packages

5. Video/computer interface

6. The computer as an exploratory tool.

7. Software evaluation and selection.

For student who wish to develop a computer science emphasis the following courses are available at WOSC.

First year

CS 101 Computers and Society 4 credits

CS 133 Computer Coding - BASIC 4 credits

Second year

Cs 211 Introduction to Computer Science 4 credits

CS 212 Techniques of Programming- PASCAL 4 credits

CS 215 Computer Organization 4 credits

CS 213 Symbolic Language- FORTRAN 4 credits

CS 217 Into to Data Processing -COBOL 4 credits

Third year

CS 311 Symbolic Language Programming 3 credits

CS 371 Applications Programming 1 3 credits

CS 372 Application Programming II 3 credits

Fourth year

CS 430 Data Structures and Management 3 credits

CS 406g Special Topics 3 to 4 credits

MTH 406g Extended BASIC 4 credits

Students who wish to become the managers and area specialists on computers within speed need to have much of the same basic training as any other computer science person on the lower division level. Their upper division work should be directed toward the area of teaching about computers or the development of instructional material. To provide for this need WOSC offers the following courses.

ED 451g Microcomputer Systems 3 credits

The building of a working vocabulary dealing with microcomputers. Essential hardware and software components and their functions are studied. Applications of microcomputer systems within the classroom are investigated.

ED 452g computer Based Education 3 credits

Characteristics of computer-based education illustrating the advantages to be derived from using computer-managed and computer-assisted interactive systems. Most of the work in the class will be focused on the microcomputer. Prior classwork in ED 451g and/or CS 133 is required.

ED 461g Computer -Assisted Instruction 3 credits

The design of computer-assisted instruction lessons and interactive systems will be studied. Students will be asked to design a set of computer-assisted lessons for classroom use.

ED 466g Computer-Managed Instruction 3 credits

This course is designed to introduce students to a computerized method of testing, record keeping, and decision making that will assist administrative, classroom, and individual learner management. The student examines how computer-managed instruction can solve the management problems of individualized instruction.

A revised education technology masters degree programming incorporating up to 18 credit hours in computer application courses has received committee approval and is in the process of being implemented.

Supporting our underlying philosophy that the computer is an instructional medium available to all students, WOSC has one central facility consisting of 13 APPLE II microcomputers, 10 of which are connected to two CORVUS hard disk drives. Two of the systems have printers attached to them. In addition there are three free standing units, one of which has a video interface. This facility is located in the college library providing access to all. There are also six microcomputers located around campus for faculty development of programmes and classroom demonstration. During the course of the school year over 50 per cent of the college population interacts with these computers.

The CAUSE Grant has allowed us, as Western Oregon State College, to begin acquainting faculty and administrators with microcomputers. The faculty has begun to examine the curriculum to see how to make use of computers as a teaching tool and to determine the degree of exposure a beginning teachers needs to be prepared for tomorrow's classroom.

Realizing that public education is in a period of dramatic change, we believe that all aspects of teacher-education must be examined to insure that we can help future teachers not only gain skills in working with people but also gain the skills needed to use the developing educational technology. Curriculum must be continually examined and adjusted or teacher education risks being out of phase with both students and society itself.

Computers for teachers activities at the university of michigan schools of education

In this report we describe the present status and future plans for computer-related activities at the School of Education. Also we hope to covey something of our approach and our ideas about helping teachers with computers in schools. The views expressed are those of the authors but many of the ideas are from others in our research collaborative for computers in education and the resource center. All contribute to the planning, research, teaching and service.

Introduction

Before listing some of the things being done for teachers using the resources of the School of Education at the University of Michigan we should describe the basis for our interest in and approach to serving education through computers. In general, we strive for balance among teaching, research and service' we hope to develop, apply and share knowledge about the use of computers at all levels of education, elementary school through college. We choose to give special attention to school and community resources, and then make the most of the special resources of the University of Michigan and the School of Education.

Focus on school and community resources. The things most important to effective learning with computers are happening today in schools and homes, not in universities and the colleges. What we do for teachers using the resources of the School of Education muse serve them well in their own schools and communities. Therefore the pre-service training, as well as in-service programmes and consolation, is carried out with an eye for the facilities and situations which will be found in the local schools.

Computers, education, and teachers.. Inexpensive computing facilities that are easy to use will be one of the more important things to happen to education in this century. We believe that she experience of teachers and the availability of technical support will be the most important factor in determining how well computers are used in schools. The need is now, and growing more rapidly than institutions are professional organizations can respond.

A role for School of education. Colleges and universities can translate interest in computers and education into actions to meet the needs of students, teachers and administrators by going out into the schools and communities to assist with operational programmes, by maintaining high standards for professional development and practice, and by nurturing appropriate interest in research, e.g., to increase knowledge about teaching and learning processes. More specifically, we recommend that schools of education provide practitioners with skills in teaching and administration of computer-related curriculum as well as information about computers, and arrange for continuing support of on-going programmes as well as one-shot training to get them started. Action-oriented research is appropriately included in all training and support activities, that is, professionals should get involved in planning for, collecting and interpreting data to aid in decisions in their schools.

Resource of the colleges and universities. Training and support offered to teachers through colleges and universities should take advantage of the special resources available there. Microcomputers are used throughout the University in many different ways: information systems, process control, laboratory equipment, specialized graphics, etc. Students have a unique opportunity to learn about current and future uses of microcomputers, and as teachers they need to know about computing in their areas, in jobs, and in society, not just in the classroom. Exploration of microcomputer applications opens doorways onto the entire world of computing.

The university of Michigan has been a leader in computers and education since a Food Foundation grant in 1956 for curriculum development in engineering education. Nearly all parts of the University have been involved, humanities and the arts as well as sciences and professions. Various unites provide courses as well as software and applications, Research and development throughout the University contributes to the quality of the programme in the School of Education, and education faculty help other units using computers in teaching give appropriate attention to matters of leaning and teaching. We believe the most effective uses of computers in education today are will based in the subjects taught and in supporting disciplines, so we do not treat "Computers in education" as a separate discipline.

Overview of this report. The first section describes the academic programmes in the School of Education: degree programmes, courses, independent work, and cooperation with other teaching units. The second and third sections summarize service and research activities. The facilities for educational computing are describe briefly in the last section, and we close with a brief statement about future directions.

Academic programmes

Graduate Degree programmes with Specialization Computers

The University of Michigan School of Education is organized in give large units: administration and policy planning: development, learning and teaching; higher science. computers are used in all the programmes, but they get particular attention in "development, learning and teaching" as part of literacy. Special topic such as problem solving, learning strategies and social relations are considered in all four areas of literacy.

Computing in education is not treated as a separate degree programme because the University gives only one masters degree or doctorate in education, and more importantly, because computing in education is considered in context rather than as a separate subject.

Courses Specific to Microcomputers in education

Microcomputers and Education provides an

overview of computers in education with special attention to instructional design, testing and evaluation. Microcomputer Programming for Educators serves as an introduction as well but leads to specific skills is one or more languages and the development of specific programmes for use in ones teaching. These two courses are offered every term and enroll about 30 students each time.

Microcomputers in the Classroom integrates programming, instructional design and classroom management. Seminar in the Use of Microcomputers in Education provides for advance project work. These two courses are scheduled once each year and restricted to graduate students; typical enrollment is 20.

Special topics for Independent Reading and Research

Because the field is growing and changing more rapidly that a school of education can respond with new courses, and because the student learning about computers in education come from varying backgrounds and situations, the College offers many opportunities for study of special topics by individuals and small groups in addition to regular courses. Typically students will define topics for independent reading or research, often derived from questions raided during one of the regular courses, and sometimes based on experiences in their own teaching, research of administration. One or more faculty members will assist in redefining the topic and identifying resources for independent work. The results often are reported through informal seminars as well as in publishable reports. About ten students use this option each year.

These opportunities for independent work provide some of the flexibility needed in an new area of study, and help determine what topics later students should study as a more formal programming is developed. That is, some of the following topics may become regular courses:

Computer use in science, match, social studies, etc.

Planning and administration of computer labs and programmes

Curriculum science and education

Information sciences and education

Social amplifications of technology

State and regional Progrmmes for computers in education

Learning theories and technology

Research and evaluation

Practicum or project experience

The need for practitioners helping with computer applications and studies in schools is considerable and immediate. The linkage between research and practice is of immediate benefit to operational programmes as well as long-term research. Therefore, practical experience is very appropriate in a graduate study of computers in education. We encourage practicums and project experience, either in association with on-going projects in the school of Education or elsewhere in the University, or in the schools in which the candidates presently work. We know no better "examination" than that provided by experience in the field: managing a microcomputer lab, developing instructional applications in one's discipline, or helping teachers to use computers more effectively in their classrooms. We expect about ten students a year to enroll for credit in a practicum; presently the only students in this category are working on doctoral dissertations.

Contributions to undergraduate courses

Undergraduates in our teacher preparation programme have ample opportunity to use computers in their regular classes or independent work. In addition to trying computer applications in the relevant discipline, students are likely to be signed other interesting activities, such as using a microcomputer to carry out a readability analysis of text materials and designing a computer-based learning activity. A microcomputer resource center provided machines, software, publications, and other materials for individual work, as well an opportunity to observe learners from pre-school to adult working with computers individually or in classes

Diffusion of computing through methods classes began with a grant from the "faculty development fund" at the Center for Research on Learning and teaching. We went to the instructors with suggestions for computer use in the various disciplines, demonstrated the applications, and offered to assist. Virtually all methods courses now include computing activity directed by the individual instructors, with technical assistance form the staff of the resources center. Students can go on to teach themselves more about computers; some enroll in the undergraduate classes.

Cooperation with other teaching units

The School of Education draws on the resources of other units that work with computers and information systems, and also coordinates its efforts with others interested in computers in schools. The School of Library Science shares resources for demonstration and research; working together, education and library science prepare students for serving a support function in the schools. The College of Engineering has set up microcomputer classrooms for undergraduate courses in programming and applications. At scheduled times these classrooms are available for demonstrations, workshops and special classes. The PET shop is available for other uses, especially for summer institutes since only a few chemistry lab sections are scheduled in the summer.

The Department of Computer and Communications Sciences helps staff several courses off campus for teachers needing a sound basis in computer science. The Department of Psychology has several laboratories working on learning and instruction using computers, providing graduate students in education access to a wider variety of research opportunities. The Center for Research on Learning and Teaching helps provide the resources for demonstration and research and in return the School of Education helps faculty elsewhere in the University explore computer applications in their own teaching and scholarly work, a task beyond the resources of the Center.

The communication among faculty using computers began with a series of workshops and "faculty seminars" organized by the Center for Research on Learning and Teaching. Later the same series was offered on the site of the resource center in the School of Education, establishing it as the new site of information and advice. The Apple users group meets-regularly at the School of Education, further identifying the resource center as a focal point for communication.

The cooperation among units been formalized as the Instructional Technology Research Lab, a collection of people and equipment distributed among various units: Center for Research of Learning and Teaching, Education, Engineering, media resources, and liberal arts. Through this association equipment and expertise can be assembled for research or service projects.

Service

In-Service training and related services

The School of Education offers many lectures, demonstrations and consultation on the use of microcomputers for schools. These include;

faculty orientation sessions;

intermediate district or country school board sessions; and community meetings.

At times faculty members help staff the planning of computer systems and curriculum to be used throughout a school or district. We are always conscious of helping share experience among organizations and agencies. For example, we helped establish a state task force on computers in schools, we work with regional resource centers in the public schools systems throughout the state, and, of course, we share software through professional associations and user groups.

The University also offers specific in-service programmes for schools system. These are scheduled for the convenience of those served and may include additional services such as:

consolation for individuals and departments

short-term loan of equipment

advice on special education facilities

information on computers and careers

resources for meeting special student needs

assistance with microcomputers in classroom management

training in use of various programming languages

advice on word processing and record keeping

development of microcomputers user groups

Because of the immediate needs of schools,

teachers and students we do as much as we can to provide information and assistance with operational programmes. For example, we offer advice and reference for:

fund raising

requipment acquisition

clubs

field trips

public library programmes

drop-in centers

curriculum librarier and programme exchange

electronic bulletin boards and "conferences"

science fair projects

parent-child courses

coordination of home and school uses of computers

newsletter and other publications

radio broadcasts, cable programmes, newspapers, etc.

Research

Research in progress and under consideration

Researchers at the University are active in a variety of studies and plan a comprehensive research programme on the use of computers in education. A microcomputer research collaborative established in the summer of 1979 has encouraged and participated in research on" attitudes and values; learning with computer assistance; social structures; and futures. CAI per se is not given much attention, but the researchers focus instead on aspects of learning, procedures for curriculum design, social context for learning, or other disciplines which contribute to effective use of computers in education.

The realities of computer use in schools for the next few years dominate research planning. For example, attention is being given to conceptualizing how a single microcomputer is best used with a group of students where the institution cannot afford enough machines for everyone individually or in pairs. The programme of research assumes more computers will be purchased for homes that for schools and so explores ways to exploit home computing for education.

Research is encouraged in many innovative uses of computers in education. Such uses include but are not limited to:

Attitudes that those using computers in education have toward:

learning

careers

educational institutions

technology in education

lifelong learning

creative activities supported by technology

family activities

Learning with computer assistance, including aspects of:

- efficiency
- effectiveness
- long-term effects
- thinking and problem solving
- learning skills
- skills for handling information

Social structure, involving:

- classroom structure and activities
- friendships
- interpersonal relations
- teacher-student relationships
- teacher role
- parent role
- implications for family

Futures research, including:

- anticipating new technology and its impacts
- assessing social implications
- shaping alternative futures

Facilities

Computer education resource center in the school of education

The computer education resource center is housed in the Instructional Strategy Services unit of the School of Education, providing an appropriate context, technical support, and ready access for students, faculty and the teaching support, and ready access for students, faculty and the teaching community to explore a new technology in education. Other programmes of the Service unit provide links with graphics, video, curriculum review, information services, and the like. Of course, other units in the schools of Education also use microcomputers in their work; students use machines in the Statistical Laboratory, the Center for Evaluation Research Training, and a special programme in education and psychology.

Both the manager and assistant manager of the resource center know the computer field well, along with their own specialities in library science. Workshops, demonstrations, and open access fit well within its domain, and the unit provides the larger context of teaching and learning.

Equipment. The lab includes at least one of each common microcomputer along with documentation and a library of applications. About seven Pet's, ten Apples, and a dozen Atari's can be assembled so that workshops and classes have one computer station for each of two terminals on time sharing systems, and one additional terminal is dedicated to special uses in graphics. Typically half of the machines are out in faculty offices or field research.

The equipment kept in the resource center is arranged about the periphery of the space for individual work but it can easily be shifted for group use of classroom demonstration. A second classroom is used when we call in extra machines. Group viewing is accommodated through use of large monitors: black and while monitors for applications which are primarily text, and colour where that is helpful to the demonstration. The same monitors are used for viewing material from videotape for more convenient use in group demonstrations as well as easy access by individuals. the resource center also has two vediodisc players, one consumer model and one industrial, for experiments with computer-controlled videodisc.

Repair Facilities. The staff person who handles other equipment for the Resource Center also takes care of computer connectors, cables, and the like. some time is required for the cleaning and repair of disk and cassette media, the diagnosis of equipment problems, and minor repairs. This person also makes arrangements for outside repair as needed.

Materials. The computer lab maintains a large set of materials in cooperation with the Center for Research on Learning and Teaching. The center manages to maintain:

a comprehensive programme library

a substantial reference library

most of the relevant periodicals

manuals for each of the machines

most of the recent textbooks

media materials

video tape

tape-slide

computer programmes

annotations on programmes and applications

self-help posters

Staffing. The resources center is supervised by experienced library and media staff. The manager, assistant manager and laboratory aides together provide service to both faculty and students: comparison of equipment options: identification and review of software: advice on development of applications: and assistance with preparation of graphics for use in papers and other presentations. That is, the resource center provides computer resources for any scholarly work by students, as well as a site for study of computers in education.

In addition to the regular staff and faculty, undergraduates are hired as aides and programmers to extend the support staff to serve more people at modest cost. At the same time, the students use their work a s a learning experience. About twenty undergraduate student benefit from this opportunity each term. Graduate students help with review application programmes and publications. Workshops, short courses and programme review are carried on by faculty members on a regular basis.

Uses outside regular instruction. Service to other

units, organizations and informal groups have proved mutually benefical. For example, the University of Michigan Apple users group meets regularly, and typically some education students who happened by, get "hooked" and leave with some new ideas of software for innovation or use.

Graduate students have gained excellent experience staffing special courses for the university Children Center, and education classes have observed young children exploring computers. The resource center is a resource for local teachers, providing the full tango of information and examples maintained for University students and faculty, and offering demonstrations in an "open house" format and instruction through institutes and workshops. In addition, and academic programme for talented students offered by the Gifted Students Institute each summer since 1978 provides one example of the "computer camp" idea that has becomes so popular recently.

3 The Role of Computers in Higher-Order Thinking

"Properly designed, can allow students to formulate hypotheses, test them, analyze results, and refine their conceptions. Moreover, they can provide the student with a record of the course of his or her investigations, permitting greater self-awareness of thinking and learning." There are, however, many barriers to realizing this potential, among them a lack of consensus on the definition of higher-order thinking and an incomplete understanding about the use of technology to promote it. We explore both issues in this chapter.

Higher - order thinking: what is it and do schools teach it?

Defining higher-order thinking

There are diverse views about the components of higher-order thinking and no adequate and agreed upon theory from which to derive a definition that would elicit consensus. Although a number of researchers have developed theories, definitions, and criteria for higher order thinking, a consensun remains elusive. For instance, Feurstein emphasizes "autonomous learning" and the importance of logical reasoning, recognizing relationships, classifying and comparing concepts. Foshay stresses the importance of learning to learn, which he labels the "pursuit of meaning," and includes such components as learning facts and findings, learning techniques, learning sources and processes interpreting information. Zacharias is more practical, emphasizing heuristics such as determining whether a problem can be solved, pushing possibilities to the limit, even to absurdity, asking for help, changing scale to achieve a different perspective, and bringing in outside information. Each perspective is valid, but they do not combine to provide a consensus.

For the purpose of this chapter, *we suggest that higher order thinking occurs when a person is engaged in active and sustained cognitive effort directed of solving a complex problem and when the person makes effective use of prior knowledge and experience in addressing the problem.* The problem must be complex for the person; many problems will meet this criterion for some people but not for others. Problems may be well-structured with clear definition, rules, and goals or ill-structured with unclear definition, ambiguous rules, and subjective goals . By *sustained effort* we mean engagements requiring anywhere from ten minutes to many hours or longer. *Cognitive effort* includes activities generally identified in the literature on problem solving, such as integrating and synthesizing different bodies of information, making critical judgments, and developing and testing hypotheses.

We include the concept of effectiveness in our definition because an important overall pedagogical goal is to improve the student's capacity to succeed in solving increasingly complex problems. We believe that a novice problem solver, although engaged in active and sustained cognitive effort, may not use strategies of the same efficiency as those used by an expert. On the other hand, an expert who very quickly reaches the correct solution to a problem that to other might be complex would not be engaged in higher-order thinking. We believe that effectiveness in higher-order thinking necessarily involves making appropriate use of prior knowledge and experience relating to the problem. This conception of higher-order thinking enables us to think about ways of realistically challenging students of different ages and with different levels of knowledge as they deal with problems they perceive to be intellectually complex.

Although we can not precisely specify the components of higher-order thinking, w have a good idea of what such thinking is not. while higher-order thinking may be involved, it usually is not evident when the central activities of students are (a) memorizing, (b) learning isolated facts and findings (c) using algorithms rigidly or automatically, or (d) answering problems with solutions already known to them. Such activities do not involve higher-order thinking because they do not represent "complex" problems nor do they require sustained cognitive effort for most students. We will argue, however, that facts, findings and algorithms are important building blocks for constructing concepts, principles, and now algorithms that may be necessary to solve complex problem.

Do schools teach higher - order thinking?

Our definition of higher-order thinking suggests that much of what goes on in schools bears only an indirect relationship to higher-order thinking. Evidence of lack of instruction in higher -order skills comes from a variety of places. Studies of reading instruction find that 90 percent of instruction is directed at the learning of isolated words and only 5 percent is focused on understanding text. Surveys of textbooks indicate the tremendous emphasis on vocabulary learning and the superficial and fragmented nature of the material. Studies of mathematics instruction report that early instruction in arithmetic may even drive our some of the effective problem-solving strategies that students bring to school. The nature of standardized achievement tests discourages teachers from focusing on higher-order skills. Items on such tests typically require responding with discrete bits of information in a multiple-choice format. Domains for these tests are often rigidly defined and rarely require students to synthesize information across defined domains.

Recent work by a small group of educators and cognitive psychologists has resulted in school-based curricula designed to improve thinking skills. Like others, Sternberg has argued for the necessity for training students to think: "Each program should provide explicit training both in the mental processes used in task performance and in self-management strategies. Techniques for teaching these skills cover a wide range of options and philosophies. Glaser and Sternberg have described and analyzed several of the more touted instructional programs and their reported successes. These programs range from teaching ways to structure problems and generalizable heuristics in a nearly content-free environment to training strategies within a specific content domain.

Can computers help?

Generally, computers software for the schools is similar to other instructional material in its focus on imparting factual information and on low-level algorithmic skills. There is evidence that students can learn factual information effectively by using computers in academic subject areas. For instance, the effectiveness of computer-aided instruction has been consistently demonstrated in foreign language and in science. Across subject areas, computerized instruction is associated with greater or equal gains in learning when compared with traditional instruction. Furthermore, this achievement is obtained in equal or less time than is needed for regular classroom learning.

An experiment carried out in the Los Angeles Unified School District shows some of th potential for computer-assisted instruction.

In conjunction with the Educational Testing

Service, the district conducted a five-years longitudinal experiment using the Computer curriculum Corporation's drill and practice software that was originally developed by Patrick Suppes. The purpose was to determine whether these computer programs could improve performance of students in compensatory education programs in mathematics, reading and language arts. Compared to a control group, students using the CAI materials showed large and significant gains. Further, the use of CAI curricula helped students to improve standardized test scores significantly. Nearly all the research on effects of computer-assisted instruction in schools focuses on knowledge development programs similar to the programs in the Los Angeles schools. Such programs account for the greatest use of computers in elementary schools.

There is little evidence however that computer software stimulates higher-level thinking. This lack of evidence is one of the reasons that software to promote higher-order thinking is used in schools only to a very limited degree. Another reason is that few programs are available, even though the quality of such programs is beginning to improve. It should also be noted that software programs which attempt to provide challenges to solve complex problems are (a) apt to require a longer a longer time for the student to complete. (b) difficult to integrate with the curriculum, (c) difficult for the teacher to master, and (d) difficult to evaluate. Nonetheless, there are computer programs and programming languages that, according to authors' claims, can improve problem-solving skills. Data assessing these claims, however, are sparse.

Programming languages that allow the student to control the computer and provide an inherently rich problem-solving environment have attracted much attention. One such programming language is Logo, developed explicitly for young children. It includes an interactive component that allows students to give directions to the computer by informing a "turtle" what to draw. The computer draws what the child has directed. This process allows for immediate feedback. Part of the advocacy for teaching even young children how to direct or program a computer results from a belief that learning to think like a computer makes a better thinker. The argument is not that thinking like a computer is somehow better than human thought, but that the consideration of thinking makes humans more thoughtful.

Researchers have compared the problem-solving performance of subjects who used such programs with the performance of those who did not, but no conclusive results have emerged. Some data suggest tat learning th Logo programming language is significantly different from learning other languages because of its interactive nature. Scattered and sparse evidence indicates that Logo instruction may have a positive influence on much things as fluency, originality, and divergent thinking. Some have hypothesized that increased facility with Logo provides the potential for improved thinking to the extent that it acts as a tool for expressing powerful ideas. By using Logo, children have the opportunity to gain a personal understanding of abstract ideas they are unlikely to encounter until a much higher level of schooling, if at all.

Evaluating claims about computer programs or language designed to improve higher-order thinking skills is a more complex process than evaluating knowledge-building programs. Definitions are not as precise and, as we have indicated, there are no agreed upon outcome measures. It is only recently that researchers have begun to prove the claims of developers for programs to improve higher-order thinking.

The use of heuristics in teaching-order thinking

One of the ways in which computer programs may possible help in developing the skills of higher-order thinking is through instruction in the use of heuristics, that is, instruction in particular strategies of problem solving. Before considering this matter, we found it useful to look into such questions as (a) Can heuristic strategies be taught and do they actually help students solve problems? an (b) Does training in such strategies transfer across various domains of content?

Can heuristic strategies be taught and do they help in problem solving?

One of the most popular views is that a way to teach higher-order thinking skills is to instruct students in particular strategies to solve problems. Simon has pointed out that "powerful general methods o exist and... they can be taught in such a way that they can be used in new domains whether they are relevant."

Perhaps the best known set of problem-solving heuristics is included in Polya's classic work *How to Solve it*. He developed four categories of heuristics: figuring out the problem, devising a plan, carrying out the plan and looking back. Feuerstein's instructional techniques to improve problem-solving skills include such activities as classifying and comparing attributes, recognizing relationships, planing, synthesizing, and logical reasoning. Lipman emphasized that it is important for students to monitor their own thinking by suing such strategies as identifying underlying assumptions, grasping whole-part and part-whole relationships, and applying principles to real-life situations.

Newell, Shaw, and Simon argued in 1960 that "heuristics are...things that aid discovery. Heuristics seldom provide infallible guidance.... Often they `work', but the results are variable and success is seldom guaranteed." Suydam, on the other hand, found that "research evidence strongly concurs that problem-solving performance is strongly enhanced by teaching students to use a wide variety of strategies of heuristics, both general and specific." The twenty years that separate these assessments account in part for the disagreement, but good data are still sparse, and the methods advocated for teaching heuristics are mainly based on common sense and intuitive understandings.

As early as 1950, researchers explored the hypothesis that students who use explicit problem-solving strategies are better problem solvers than those who do not and that such strategies can be taught so that skills are improved. Bloom and Broder investigated the problem-solving skills of college students across a variety of subject areas. They found that bright students who were poor problem solvers could be trained to improve their problem-solving skills using the strategies employed by peers who were successful problem solvers. These who participated in the training tended to score. 49 to .68 grade levels higher than matched groups with no training. They also expressed confidence and optimism about their newly learned problem-solving abilities.

More recently, Ptt found that specific instruction that followed the four-step heuristics of Polya's model was effective in improving fifth graders' use of the strategies, but he did not find significant differences in success in solving problems between the experimental group and a control group that had no training. Since the period of treatment was only four weeks, it is nt surprising that problsm-solving outcomes were not dramatically influenced. In another study, fourth graders who were taught to develop pictorial aids, such as tables and diagrams, could solve more problems than others who did not receive such instruction.

Within the area of mathematics, instruction in problem solving heuristics is generaly spplied to clearly structured problems. schoenfeld successfully trained college-level students to use specific techniques to improve their strategie for solving work problems in algebra. In a follow-up project, Schoenfeld reported that not only did college level students increase their use of particular strategies, but those who used the heuristics effectively wer also more successful at solving algebra problems. Perhaps as a result of this success, the students' self-reprts of their problem-solving skills were more favorable. In another study on solving word problems in algebra, Mayer and Bovenmeyer found that performance was predicted by ability to underatand the problem and plan the solution.

In summary, weak but promising data suggests that heuristics can be taught and that their use improves students' problem-solving abilities.

Does training in problem-solving strategies transfer across various domains of content?

Some researchers believe that effective problem-solving strategies are specific to particular domains. The argument is that a student gets deeper into a content domain the problem solving skills become more and more specific to that modain and therefore may not transfer to other domains

Studies of expert and novice problem solvers are particularly salient here. These studies have found that when novices and experts are faced with a problem in the experts' domain, they pproach the problem in different ways. Novices tend to focus on the litral objects defined in th statement of the problem. The possible strategies for solution seen by experts are expanded by their uderstanding of the relationships among concepts and procedures specific to that domain.

How are we to reconcile the findings of these expert-novice studies with the views of those who see the value of generalized problem-solving heuristics across different subject matters? One line of argument is simply that increased knowledge of a content domain makes possible a more efficient and precise application of general heuristic procedures. Greater knowledge of a domain should increase the chances fora person to define a problem accurately, allow on to decide more easily among possible strategies for solution and facilitate resting the validity of possible solutions. In this argument, procedural problem-solving skills interact with the knowledge base to increase the abilities of the student to solve the problem. We might imagine a model with three significant effects: two main effects and an interaction effect of the two.

Drawing from observational studies of students, recent researchers have considered this issue. In a detailed analysis of problem solving in geometry, Greeno argued that three kinds of knowledge are critical for success: (a) heuristic knowledge necessary for carrying out proofs, such as setting goals, forming plans, and generally organizing the problem-solving process; (b) knowledge of specific geometiric facts, such as the definition of lines and angles; (c) geometric concepts essential to making inferences and proving theorems. Similarly, Glaser and Pellegrino concluded that two critical and interreleated components are necessary for higher-order thinking to occur: (a) thoughtful consideration of 'procedural constraints of a particular problem area, such as inductive or analogical reasoning," as problem-solvig tools and (b) subject area knowledge.

Recent rheoretical work in cognitive sciences has used the notion of knowledge structure or schemata to help explain the way people remember, comprehend, and solve problems. Schema theory attempts to describe the relationships between knowledge previously acquired, the way it is organized in the mind, and the ease with which new knowledge is acquired and used. Experts re viewed as having rich and complex schema that facilitate the acquisition of new information and the rapid solution of many problems. The prior knowledge base and schema of the expert in physics is sufficiently rich so that many high school physics problems can be solved algorithmically. The expert "knows" the way to define the problem, "knows" the right strategy to solve it, and "knows" how to evaluate the solution. He may apply Polya's steps but he will do so unconsciously and rapidly; for him this is rotine processing, not higher-order thinking. To a high school student with a less complete knowledge schema in physics, however, the same problem may pose a complex task requiring higher-order thinking. Although the student may have a solid base of facts and an understanding of the basic rules of physics, the probvlem may require combining the facts and rule in novel ways. The student may have to examine multiple ways of representing the problem and explorea variety of possible will be engaged in higher-order thinking ony when they are stretched beyond situations where tey already know how to find the solution. It also implies that constant deepenig of a subject area to include increasingly complex material is critical for either students of experts as they deal with tasks that require higher-order thinking.

Psychologists investigating metacognition suggest that students who self-consciously consider their own cognitive procssing can enhance their thinking. Much recent research indicates that the student is very active in selecting, interpreting, and even altering the content of instruction. The key processes seen as integral to effective monitoring of cognition are (a) planning activities prior to undertaking a problem (b) monitoring activities during learning and checking outcomes. These activities are remarkably similar to Polya's heuristics and they also reflect Papert's argument for teaching children to program computer. Controlled use of Polya's heuristic strategies may be viewed as an example of the regulation of cognition. Brown postulated that individuals have a centrl processing unit, much like a computer, that controls heuristic routines for problem solving, planning and scheduling appropriate strategies, and monitoring and evaluating the effects of strategies. The complex operations performed by the executive control component take one of two approaches automativ or controlled. Automatic strategies are quickly retrived, make little demand on the cognitive system, require minimal conscious learner control, and are not dependent on short-term memory. controlled strategies are more slowly retrieved, executed in a deliberate, purposeful way, and thus require a great deal of lerner effort and control. Controlled strategies can evolve into automatic operations. For example, if Polya's heuristics are practiced in a controlled, conscious way across a number of problem areas, there is reason to believe that their application will become automatic.

This discussion has implications for school curricula intended to encourage higher-order thinking. First, for students to find new ways of interrelating knowledge and algorithms they must have a firm grasp of the knowledge needed to solve the problem. If they cannot retrieve this information automatically, they will be distracted from the problem-solving task. Second, if students are to be challenge with higher-order problems at various stages of their knowledge development in a field, then the curriculum should not be organized hierarchycally to focus initialy only on learning facts and formulas. Instead, students should be challenged to solve problems earlky in their exposure to a field-problems based on the knowledge they have already acquired. Considerable attention should be given early in the curriculum to the interrelatinship among facts and rules in order to develop schema that are sufficiently rich to enable students to deal with problems that require organizing informatin in ways new to them. The selection of content for early problem-solving activities is therefore particularly important.

In addition to depth in a single content area, repeated successful experience in using problem-solving strategies across a variety of content ares reinforces learners' use of them in new situations they recognize as resembling the ones in which they succeeded. Psychologists endorse training in multiple contexts because it "decreases the likelihood that a particular piece of information will be wedded to a particular context." If students assume that solving a problem requires the use of a formula or algorithm applicable only in a single subject area, then they will use these strategies only within that domain. But, if they see problems requiring heuristic strategies and other substrative concepts across a number of domains, it is likely that they will become more fluid thinkers and, ultimately, more successful in solving problems.

Our brief literature review suggests the importance of teaching heuristic strategies, that using these strategies in a rich context enhances their effectiveness, and that there is some evidence that strategies may be transferable across content domains. Summarizes out major conclusions about problem solving and the appropriate context, with accompanying citations on work in the area.

The analysis indicates that students can learn problems-solving heuristics and that, if they use these strategies, they are more effective problem solvers. The instructional emphasis should be on the process of solving problems and not on the problem solution. One implication of this focus on process is the need for students to practice using heuristic strategies across a variety of content domains and with different types of problems.

The depth of the content appears to be a critical component in improving higher-order thought. Research on expert and novice problem solvers show the importance of a solid information base that is easily retrieved in a problem-solving environment. The problem solver should be able to retrieve facts and algorithms automatically, but should also be able to perceive the interrelationships among various concepts within a domain.

Analysis of computer software for teaching higher-order thinking

We turn now to an examination of some existing software that may be used to develop higher-order thinking skills. We have organized out discussion of this software under the following topics:

(1) Software to develop knowledge and skills (drill and practice programs, content tutorials, heuristic tutorials; (2) Problem-solving simulations; (3) Aids to problem solving. In our comments about various software items we not their particular characteristics and we use ideas from the previous section on higher-order thinking

to suggest how the software could be improved to enhance its usefulness in promoting the development of such thinking.

Programs to develop knowledge and skills

There are conflicting opinions about the use in schools of computer programs which "only" provided drill and practice or tutorial instruction. One view s that these activities can be carried out by teachers or aids effectively and cheaply and that we use of such programs limits students' and teachers' various on the power of computers and reinforces the already strong emphasis in schools on knowledge development to the exclusion of problem-solving activities. Another view is that such programs can be easily integrated into the curriculum, that they can free the teacher for more demanding activities, that they have been shown to be effective, that they often command the attention of some students more than does conventional teaching and that they offer a convenient way to introduce computers into the classroom.

We favor the latter view, though we quickly concede that many existing programs in these categories are not worth students' time and effort. Moreover, the attention in the early part of this chapter to the need for exposure to content depth and for facility of retrieval of knowledge and algorithms as prerequisites for solving complex problems reinforces our view that the knowledge development programs can serve a very useful purpose.

Drill and practice software focuses on previously learned factual knowledge and skills, in contrast, the other two types of knowledge development software focus on learning new knowledge or skills. Drill and practice software is used with greater frequency in schools than any other types of program, other than programming languages. Over the past few years the aesthetic quality and the motivational attributes of these programs have improved greatly as program developers have acquired sophistication in the use of graphics and have learned something about how to design programs that sustain the attention of young people.

Properly constructed drill and practice programs should enhance cognitive processing by requiring students to increase speed in retrieving information and in carrying out skill activities to the point where these activities become automatic. This automatic processing, in turn, should assist higher-order thinking by reducing certain cognitive demands on students when they are faced with a problem- solving situation. The goal is to get students to the point where they can focus on the dimensions of the problem rather than on the heuristics to solve it.

One approach is to have the software deliberately focused on increasing student's speed in processing information. Unlike drill and practice activities that require only paper and pencil, a computer program can record the time it takes a student to carry out a problem or to remember or recognize certain information. In addition, it can adjust the amount of time required to present a problem, based on its record of how quickly similar tasks were complete. Finally, criterion levels can be developed experimentally to assess whether students have achieved the skills to carry out th task automatically.

A second approach would be to design programs to increase the student's capacity to "chunk: together related pieces of information. The ability to solve problems is partially constrained bay the amount of information a person can manipulate in short-term or immediate memory. The capacity of human short-term memory is limited to a small and finite number of independent pieces of information-in the neighborhood of seven. If students could automatically chunk together pieces of information so that the pieces are no longer independent, they might be able to increase their ability to solve complicated problems. Based on some assumption about the structure and extent of students' knowledge schema, drill and practice programs might be designed to help them bring together or "chunk" related information.

Content tutorial programs differ from drill and practice programs by focusing on new facts and skills rather than on going over material already learned or partially learned. Typical software resembles some of the early teaching maching programs with dry presentation of desecrate information and only a limited branching capacity. Many of the early tutorial programs developed by the Minnesota Education Computing Consortium are of this sort. More interesting tutorial performance could challenge the student to become involved through game-like situations, The tole of these programs in enhancing problem solving is to provide sufficient grounding in content and skill areas so that complex problems can be presented.

The ETS-LAUSD study and other reports indicate that programs in this category can be very successful in teaching information and skills. The quality and sophistication of this type of program have also increased dramatically over the years. Their demonstrated ability to engage students, particularly low-achieving students, is a good reason to make them available in more schools. Nonetheless, or earlier review of the literature suggests a variety of ways to improve the usefulness of content tutorial programs for preparing a student to solve complex problems.

As in the case of drill and practice programs, the concept of chunking has been neglected and might be used to enhance effectiveness. Two strategies that could aid in chunking are (a) the use of mnemonic devices, and (b) semantic mapping. The first strategy is often used to facilitate the learning of lists of apparently unrelated objects. Pictures as well as key words can be useful. Semantic mapping is closer theoretically to the notions of cognitive scientists who perceive the ability to chunk as characteristic of "expert" thinking. It is designed to aid the individual to develop cognitive structures, or schema, to organize new knowledge. In semantic mapping, new concepts are systematically related to already known concepts in order to place the new information into a familiar structure or context.

Using semantic mapping as a model for teaching new content would require that the computer program acquire information about the prior knowledge of students in order to relate new information to familiar concepts. Here the computer new information to familiar concepts. Here the computer is at a distance disadvantage when compared to a human teacher; not even the most powerful electronic brains comes close to the capacity of the human brain to make judgments about students' previous experience and to tailor information to meet special group and individual needs.

Nonetheless, we can imagine tutorial programs that initially interrogate a student to determine a general level of prior knowledge and then use the results of the interrogation to tailor the tutorial to student needs. Where schools knowledge is ordinarily learned in a hierarchical manner as in mathematics, the computer could pretest and then use responses to place students at the appropriate level in the tutorial. In areas where knowledge is not clearly hierarchical, the initial assessment would be complicated and require greater teacher involvement.

A related way to improve tutorial programs is through the use of diagnostic routines that identify the type of errors that students make and then coach or instruct them in ways to avoid making such errors. This strategy appears to be particularly useful for learning skills such as arithmetic operations. The classing example of such a program is BUGGY, a diagnostic program to detect the nature of errors made by students doing subtraction problems. In its original form it identified a very large number of possible independent error patterns, though the actual errors that students made tended to cluster in far fewer patterns. This software was initially written for a large computer but it being modified for microcomputers.

The small amount of quickly accessed memory is still a general problem for developing effective instructional software for microcomputers. But the BUGGY experience suggests that programs containing a diagnostic and coaching component may need to include only the most frequently occurring errors. Ideally, the program would instruct a student to request teacher assistance if it could not determine the student's error. This would free teachers to focus on the most complex instructional problems.

Cognitive scientists have recently observed the phenomenon of systematic misconceptions in the areas of science and mathematics. In the early grades these misconception have only minor consequences for "getting the answer right" and therefore persist into later education, where they could have considerable influence on the problem-solving abilities of students. It should be possible to design computer programs that systematically test for prevalent misconceptions and then provide coaching routines to heop overcome them.

Heuristic tutorial programs are specifically designed to teach problem-solving strategies. These computer programs use a well-structured and circumscribed, often game-lime environment for training and practice in the use of specific heuristics.

The classic computer programs in this area is the game of "Wumpus", which was designed to teach basic knowledge of logic, probability, decision analysis, and geometry to a wide range of learners, from young children to adults. The game logic resolves around a set of five basic rules of reasoning. The player is placed randomly in a connected web of vaves and is told the neighbors of his current location. The goal is to locate the horrible wumpus and kill it by shooting an arrow into its lair. Moving from one cave to another produces information on the new neighbors. Players can minimize dangers and make progress in finding the Wumpus by using the. warning signals to make appropriate ligistc and probalistics inferences. If the players exhaust their supply of five arrows before killing the Wumpus, the game is lost.

We believe schools and most programs developers are missing major opportunity by not developing and using programs like "Wumpus" Properly developed programs could be used on a regular basis in schools with students of widely varying background to provide them with systematic exposure to problem-solving situations. For instance, the Sunburst Corporation has published a problem-solving skill matrix that is included with software packages designed to teach complex thinging skills such as discrimination, looking for a pattern, and information gathering. Generally, these computer programs are open-ended and create a fantasy environment. For instance, in "Memory Castle." students learn mnemonic systems by playing an adventure game that leads them through a castle, and they must use a special code to find the way out. in another program, "The pond", a small green fraog, lost in a pond of lily pads, teaches students to recognize an articulate patterns and generalize from raw data. The student chooses from six ponds, or levels of difficulty, in which lily pads are displayed in increasingly complex patterns. The objective is to determine which pattern can get the frog across the pond. A second level of the game encourages students to collect points by directing frogs through as many points as possible in the fewest number of moves.

There is little question in our minds that these programs ares successful in teaching students to use specific problem-solving heuristics within the limited program environments, but we know of no quantitative evaluations. And whether the strategies learned from these programs have effects that generalize to other settings, particularly those where the problems are more complex or less well-structured, in another matter.

Improvements in these programs might proceed along some of the same lines that we have suggested for content tutorial and drill and practice programs. The use of error diagnosis and coaching routines seems especially promising. Burton and Brown used this strategy in a modification of a well-known arithmetic game programs, "WEST", originally developed for the PLATO system. They included routines which contrast the player's moves with optional strategies and which occasionally suggest alternative moves to the player. Once again, however, we know of no systematic, controlled evaluation.

Problem-solving simulations

The task of problem-solving simulation programs is to pose complex problems for solution. Unlike knowledge-building programs, which provide practice in sing knowledge and skills and which teach students facts and how to use certain heuristics, simulation programs present situations where the problem itself needs to be identified, where there may be a large variety of possible heuristics to use, and where there may indeed be a number of acceptable solutions. To present such a situation, the computer simulation must assume or create an environment with a sufficiently rich knowledge base and structure so that complex problems can be posed.

Paper has labelled this idea "microworld" and defended it as a subset of reality or constructed reality that allows learners to exercise powerful ideas and intellectual skills. The use off a microworld is based on a learning theory that promotes active exploration in an environment that is sufficiently limited and thus conductive to constructure exploration and at the same time rich enough for discovery.

We pointed out earlier that such a requirement creates a very difficult problem for computer programs because of the difficulties in assessing sufficient levels of students' prior knowledge and the limited memory of the microcomputer. The limitation on memory, for example, reduces the computer's capacity to communicate easily with students, for only a small vocabulary and a simplified syntax can be stored in a microcomputer. One approach is for the program to build an environment based directly on the curriculum or the common real-life experiences of students, thereby reducing the effects of difference in prior knowledge. A second option is a computer-created artificial environment where the effects of the prior knowledge of the student are minimized. Both of these approaches are described here.

Content simulation programs are designed to provide environments as lifelike as possible for students to use in problem-solving activities. A substantial number of existing computer programs do this in a sophisticated way. Programs that pose diagnostic problems in medicine, automobile care, or business management are widely used outside precollegiate education. Unfortunately, much of the content would be inappropriate for elementary and secondary schools, and many of these programs are on large computers rather than on microcomputers and therefore not generally accessible to schools. But they can serve as a vision of what is possible.

One prototype is the "MYCIN" system, an interactive program that simulates a medical consultant who specializes in infectious diseases. For approximately twenty minutes, the program questions and responds to doctors seeking the help of a specialist. They may ask "MYCIN" for advice on identifying organisms and prescribing drugs and, further, to explain that advice. This program strikes us as particularly salient in at least three ways. First, it allows the physicians to lean more about the complexities of diseases and treatments outside their specialities. Second, the encyclopedic function embedded in explaining treatments in an option and not a necessary step in using the program. Third, it allows for improvements in the system as new information becomes available- it can always be current. It is not difficult to see how this model might be followed in training students in a variety of content domains.

There are, however, few good examples in education and little use of content simulation programs in schools. Two classic simulations for use in elementary schools have been developed by MECC: "Lemonade", where the students manage a lemonade stand and earn or lose money based on their decisions; and "Oregon Trail," where a student acts as the head of a wagon train in the middle 1800s. These simulations are popular as demonstration devices but typically are not integrated into the curriculum.

At the high school level there have been some interesting new programs, but they only scratch the surface. For instance, "Revolutions: Past, Present and Future," developed by Focus Media, was designed to teach high school students a model for understanding the development of revolutionary movements. Students build their own model of events leading to a revolution following a computer comparison of the American, French, and Russian revolutions. This program is particularly appealing because the objectives include both process and content variables.

Another example is "South Dakota", an economics simulation developed by Educational Activities. It is designed to give students an understanding of variables affecting a framer's success. As a grain farmer, the student has a farm of 150 acres on which to survive for ten years and, ideally, make a profit. The student must make decisions in choosing the kind of grain to plant, hiring help to plant and harvest the crop, providing for family needs, paying taxes, and keeping the bank satisfied. In attractive feature of this program is that it can be used individually or in groups. If used in groups, the programs requires students to pool their information to succeed.

The limitation on memory is one reason for the lack of useful software in this area. the program needs to be fast and rich enough in content to overcome major differences in the prior knowledge of different students in the classroom. One approach to the memory limitation problem would be to build into the simulation itself tutorial software that could be interrogated by students seeking data or other information, such as the technical terms needed to solve some of the problems posed in the simulation. Similarly, drill and practice programs could be embedded in the simulation program. Error detection and coaching routines could be part of the simulation programs and could, in face, trigger the programs to indicate to the student the need for a tutorial or for a drill and practice experience. These "helping" programs could be designed as part of the simulation "game" though every student need not use them. Designed in this way, they would not have to be carried permanently in immediate memory. This use should reduce the effects of students' prior knowledge.

Other strategies to overcome school-based problems seem plausible. It is not entirely possible to control time demands, for the very task of solving a complex problem may require considerable time, but it is possible for the computer to save a simulation until later, and advantage that could help fit higher-order thinking tasks into fifty-minutes time slots.

The biggest problem is to integrate simulations into the curriculum; it solution would require the acceptance and use of both the computer and problem-solving activities in the classroom. We actually feel quite pessimistic about whether this will occur to a substantial degree in the next ten to twenty years; the conservative nature of the major textbook publishers and the tremendous inertia inside classroom work directly against it.

Nonetheless we have a number of suggestions about approaches that might be taken. One strategy would be to create first-class simulations that focus on content in areas outside the mainstream of academic life in schools. The vocational education are is a prime example; programs that pose problems in aircraft and automobile mechanics, in structural design, and in business management already exist and could be used in many schools. Art, music, health, and the chess club are other areas for which simulation programs are either already developed and used or easily could be. These areas may be able to respond to the new technology more creatively than academic areas in part because their knowledge domains are better defined and in part because they are less bound by tradition. This tactic might also enliven the curriculum in these areas.

If we continue the logic about well-defined knowledge domains, the first academic areas to tackle would be mathematics and science. In both of these areas the national concern over the quality of the curriculum, pedagogy, and the teachers could work infavor of using some high-quality programs. Mathematics, for example, will be a fertile field for simulation programs that pose problems in statistics, probability, and data analysis, if the recommendation of a number of the national mathematics groups are adopted. In science, the potentially useful simulation situations seem limitless.

Artificial environment simulations generate a make-believe world with a sufficiently rich knowledge base and set of rules of that complex problems can be poosed by the programs. Their capacity both to tutor and to pose problems in an integrated fashion allow them to control the influence of prior knowledge; this control enables the computer to provide successively deeper information and more complex problems. A wide variety of types of programs fits out general conception of this category. These include fantasy adventure games such as the "ZORK" series, science fiction games such as "World Builders", and complex artificial problem steeings such as "Rocky's Boots". One such program, "Robot Odyssey I" is both a simulation and an adventure game. Students can either construct a simulated robot or work through and adventure game that teaches the basic of digital electronic. Players design, build, and test robotes in a parts laboratory and tutorials assist students in all stages of the game. The problems posed by these programs, in our view, often are of equal or greater complexity and take more ingenuity and preservenacne to solve than the most difficult problems posed in schools.

Programs like these could present problems of varying complexity, designed to build on themselves in a regular fashion, and include systematic tutorial, diagnostic, and coaching systems to help students. The task of designing effective programs, however, is probably minor compared to the challenge of concinving schools and the general public that problem-solving activities in artificial domains have merit and that time could be allocated for student use of these programs.

The best of these programs are immensely popular in the home computing market and used almost not at all in schools. The reasons for the lack of use in schools are clear-they do not fit into the curriculum, they take a long time to run, and they seem frivolous since they are not based on real-life circumstances and are often advertised as games. In particular, adventure games seem most likely to be overlooked. We have observed student pursuing these programs and we have little doubt that such games motivate students and engage them in sustained cognitive activity, whether they are working individually or cooperatively. We have seen students with serious reading difficulties. Who rarely read printed material, spend extended periods working on adventure games that interact with users only in a narrative format. We know of no research on the effects of these games, but the motivation, the opportunity to control the environment, and the objectivity of the feedback appear to make them powerful teaching devices.

Aids to problem solving

The knowledge development and problem-solving

simulation programs exert considerable control over the activities of the student using he program. Problem-solving aids, on the other hand, contain programs that require the student to use them in ways and will help solve problems which may be either self-defined or externally assigned.

These programs, moreover, can be embedded in problem-simulation programs to help students to obtain information or to analyze data. We have included a large variety of programs in this category and have divided them into two general types: (a) tools for obtaining information or structural problems situations, and (b) programming languages.

Problem-solving aids are widely used in homes and schools, often for obtaining and structuring information for presentation or for aiding gin solving relatively *ell-structured* problems. In our experience it is rare that tools are used in schools to aid in solving ill-defined problems. Thus, for example, a data management system will be used in a school setting to display some data on a chart rather analysis. Or students will be given very highly structured problems in a programming course rather than be asked to design and program solutions to problems of their own choosing or that ar deliberately ill-defined. The exception may be when the aids are used deliberately to facilitate complex problem solving in advanced placement course for high school mathematics and computer programming.

Tools for aiding problem solving include some

of the most imaginative, interesting, and well-developed programs now available for the microcomputer. One reason is that many of them are simply elegant extensions on the microcomputer of tools that already exist in many schools, homes, and businesses; for example, world processing programs function as sophisticated typewriters. Another reason is that these programs are usable over and over by the same person and therefore are cost-effective. In contrast, an adventure program, upon being solved, loses its usefulness to the solver.

One class of these programs, which might deserve a separate category, is designed to facilitate writing. In terms of frequency of use in schools and homes, word processing programs, such as "Bank Street Writer", outstrip just about all other classes of programs. The growing group of ideas or outline processors is also becoming very popular; they contain a variety of routines to help a writer organize and reorganize textual information. The use of these programs in schools parallels both the emerging literature on the close relationship between writing and higher-order thinking and the recent emphasis on the need to improve writing in the schools. As these programs become familiar to classroom teachers as writing aids, additional features can be added. For example, it should be possible in the future to combine the organizational aids of idea processes with routines which prompt students with question and information on topics related to he curriculum to encourage their writing.

Other tools in this category include dictionaries, information retrieval systems , and data management systems. In the context of out general discussion of software for problem solving, each of these tools could be viewed as standing along to provide information or assistance in carrying our analysis or could be embedded into problem-solving simulation programs. We might imagine a workstation of the future similar to "Dynabank" developed at Xerox Parc several years ago. As student would sit at a computer terminal and have control over an information retrieval system containing a s much information as the Library of Congress and the data-analysis power of any modern mainframe computer. It would included capabilities for music composition and graphic arts. The computer could pose a variety of types of problems for the student, provide diagnosis and coaching, encourage the student to enter into a drill and practice or tutorial mode, and keep continuous track of student progress. All of the components of such workstation exist.

Programming languages are essential programs that require their operators to define and solve their own problems within the specific constraints of the language and the general constraints of a computer. Although we have classified programming languages as an aid for solving problems, learning to use the programming language is itself a form of problem solving. Without question, the act of solving programming problem often meets our definition of higher-programming problem often meets our definition of higher-order thinking. But whether learning to program enhances a child's general facility in solving problems in another issues.

Perhaps the view which links learning to programming with the development of higher-order thinking will wither away in the same way that the theories linking the leaning of Latin with complex reasoning have not survived. Computer programming languages, like playing chess, may be too highly stylized and structured to provide training that can be generalized to very different domains, especially those domains with more complex and ambiguous rules. On the other hand, programming provides the opportunity for combining discrete elements to equal a whole concept, a gestalt. And this is a necessary skills for solving some problems. We indicated earlier that this literature is very thin and inconclusive.

The most widespread use of programming languages in the content areas in in mathematics, where languages such as FORTRAN aid students in leaning how to formulate and solve problems. This is just the beginning of content-based programming languages. There are already sophisticated programming languages and enable students to concentrate on the form and content of subject matter as they composes music and design aesthetically pleasing and structurally sound buildings. In the future we find imagine similar metalanguages designed to enhance the problem - solving skills and the level of understanding of students in subject matter areas such as chemistry, physics, or even the social sciences and history.

4 Computer-Based Learning

The field of study: Computers in education

The impact of computers

Before we get down to the detailed study of computes as instructional media, let us get a clear overall view of the impact that computers have had on education and on training. This is, in fact, much more than the computer's potential to deliver instruction. The major impact of the proliferation of computers in just about all walks of life, has been on the *content* of education and training, rather than on the methods. As more and more people use computers in their work, it has become necessary to include instruction about computers and computing in more and more courses.

The three waves of information technology

Seigel and Davis refer to three 'waves' of the technology and the related know-how. The first wave was related to the new technology itself-the design and programming of computers and computer applications. This involved a relatively small proportion of the population. Who required highly technical, job-specific training in the sciences of computing and programming. The second wave came with the advent of the cheap microcomputer and its use by a much greater section of the population. This led to a 'hobbyist' approach to computing, everyone 'having a go' at programming and the growth of a movement in education towards 'computer literacy' for everyone. Finally, the 'third wave' is characterized by the permeation f all sectors of social and professional activity by computer systems. This wave brings with it the need for a variety of new skills and attitudes, which will enable us to use their tools and systems efficiently, without necessarily being expect in the skills of programming, or having any specialist knowledge of computer science. In this 'third wave' people will use computes as today they use cars or television sets or telephones. They have to acquire the specialist knowledge and skills to control the equipment and get the best possible performance out of it, but they do not expect to have to fix it when it malfunctions, or devise new applications for it. They just acquire the equipment that is designed for the task they wish to perform learn to use it efficiently and if it breaks down, or their requirements expand beyond the equipment's present capabilities, they call in a specialist. This image of three consecutive 'waves' is useful in the educational computing context, as it illustrates the different, and changing, requirements for education and training *about* computers. We might refer to this as 'computer as content's in contrast to our main interest in this book in 'computers as instruments' in the education or training process. We shall no pursue very deeply this discussion of computers as something to learn about, other than to indicate that probably this part of the overall field will have a greater influence on change in education than the use of computers as something to learn *with*.

Computers as content of education and computers as tools in education

We might also add that the two are to some extent inseparable. A good example is the effect on teaching methods that the mere existence of word processing, spreadsheets and database management software is already having. In most universities it is quite rate for students to type out their work on conventional typewriters. Soon, work processors will be as common in the secondary schools. As students become more skilled in the use of this tool, the way they think about written assignments is changing. Once written, a page or a paragraph is a block of information that has an entity of its own. It may be shifted about and pasted in at will. Experimental composition and rewriting become painless. What is written once, for one assignment, becomes easily usable as a component of a future paper. And why not? The student wrote it once and it has become part of his or her store of knowledge-the difference is that now a part of that store is not in the student's head, but in an external knowledge base on a diskette.

Describing the field

It is our view of the 'field' of discussion in respect

of computers and education. Our field is divided into two main sectors, which we may call 'informatics as content of education' and 'informatics as an instrument of education'. This distinction separates the problems of designing curricula for computer specialists or for general computer literacy, from the problems of utilizing computers in the educational process. Interesting and important as the first of these two sectors is, we shall not be able to devote time and space to it in this book. Our aims her are concerned with the use of computers as an instrument of education. We have divided this sector of the field into three sub-sectors, dealing respectively withe the use of computers as an administrative tool, as a tool to assist the teacher and as a tool to assist the teacher and as a tool to assist the learner-we prefer to call it a learner's tool for the learner may use the computer to help him learn or to take over routine tasks and thus reduce the drudgery of the learning process.

CAI or CAL

Alongside the specific examples of applications of computers in education, we have placed some brackets to indicate how we are using the three principal technical terms *CAL, CAI* and *CML*. Our usage does not necessarily agree with that of all other authors. Indeed, every author seems to h ave his own definitions and classifications for the same technical terms. One marked difference is in the use of the terms 'instruction' and 'Learning' on either side of the Atlantic. In the USA particularly, the term 'Instruction' tends to be used in a more global sense, for any type of teacher/learner interchange, whereas in Britain the term CAI has of late become restricted to 'programmed instruction' types of exercises' the preferred generic term being 'computer-assisted learning'. It seems that Canada, caught between the two influences, cannot make up its mind, although recent publications, such the *The elements of* CAL *suggest that perhaps the British view-that learning may be assisted in many diverse ways but only some of them have the characteristics of true* instruction-seems to be gaining ground.

However, detailed differences exist between the usage of CAL/CML/CAI in the works of British authors, even though they do agree that CAI is a subset of CAL. Some consider CMI as a variety of CAL. After all, the continuous formative evaluation f a student's progress and the feedback of the results, either to improve course materials, select different options or merely to inform the student of his progress/errors/weaknesses is one very effective way of assisting the learning process. Others exclude CML/CMI as a separate category, not a part of CAL in the strict sense. For Godfrey and Sterling, the development of a CML element is part and parcel of the development of any CAL materials. Nicholas Rsushby, on the other hand, in his book An Introduction to Educational Computing, seems to separate these two modes, dealing with them in quite distinct chapters. He also differs from us slightly n other aspects of technology, using a four-paradigm classification of *CAL:*

1. The *instructional* paradigm.

2. The *revelatory* paradigm.

3. The *conjectural* paradigm.

4. The *emancipatory* paradigm and also its use for 'serendipity' learning, or the 'browsing' through databases without clearly defined specific objectives.

The 'Tutor, Tool, Tutee' Model

Various authors have presented somewhat different schemata for organizing the different ways in which computers are being used in education and training, A simple but very useful classification was used by Taylor in his book The computer in the school: TUTOR, TOOL, TUTEE, Taylor's TUTOR category includes most of the applications listed in our 'tool for TEACHING' sub section. His TOOL category is equivalent to our 'tool for the LEARNER to SIMPLY of DELEGATE tasks'. His TUTEE category includes most of the applications we would include in in 'tools for the LEARNER to THINK WITH', especially the programming of computers in order to gain a deeper understanding of a given problem solving strategy or knowledge domain. In the remainder of this book, we shall occasionally use the 'tutor, tool, tutee' classification schemata. Note, however, that Taylor's classification does not include the upper sub-section of our schema; the use of the computer to manage the instructional process. This is because Taylor's schema is set up from the viewpoint of the learner-for example, the 'tutee' category contains *applications in which the* learner 'teachers the computer and in this sense the computer becomes the learner's 'tutee'. Our schema is set up from multiple viewpoints-learner's, instructor's and managers.

Yet another model

To close, we might mention Kearsley's classification. When discussing computer-based training, he divides the field into CMI, CAI and CAL as follows:

- CMI-Computer-Managed Instruction, which includes all the routine data processing tasks that an instructor might wish to have performed to assess students, revise materials.
- CAL-Computer-Assisted Instruction, which includes drill-and-practice, tutorial and Socratic but not testing and
- CAL-Computer-Assisted Learning, which is taken to include simulations and games, database search/Inquiry methods and programming of computers. Note that this classification uses similar terminology with quite different meanings from our own. Kearsley's use of 'CAL', is quite different. Whereas, CAI is seen as a sub-set of a much broader category termed CAL; he uses these two terms as mutually exclusive sub-categories of computer-based training, or, presumably, education.

The other difference concerns the breadth of the concept of 'instruction', Kearsley's categories imply that simulations and games and database-search exercises are not examples of 'instructional' materials. We defined the term 'instruction' somewhat more broadly. Whereas some existing examples of these type of computer applications would not qualify to be considered instructional systems or system components, there are many that do qualify to be thus classified.

Let us come back to earth, however, from these rather philosophical comments, to stress that the reader might come across a variety of classification system in the literature, but the example applications being classified are in all cases the same. Let us proceed, therefore, to an analysis of the most common types of applications.

The computer as instrument for learning

Computer-managed instruction

Computer-managed instruction can best he defined as the use of computer programmes for the on-line management of the instructional process. This may include the planning, organizing, controlling and evaluation functions as they occur during the instructional process. I stress the word during, to exclude the planning and organizing that occurs in the early stages of the instructional design/development process and the controlling and evaluation that occurs at the macro level after a particular course of instruction has been given. We are restricting CMI to the management of the teaching/learning process.

Built-in or Stand-alone CMI

CMI is not a recent concept. Indeed, the use of the

computer to store, analyse and interpret data about a process is a very typical type of application. No wonder that CMI was one of the first applications of computing to the instructional process. Note that CMI can be an integral feature of a computer-assigned or administered instructional system, or it can be a 'stand-alone' application of computer-based management of more or less conventional classroom instruction. As such, it may use an existing computer, installed for other data processing purposes, to assist the classroom teachers in the management of their courses.

Built-in

Almost all serious CAI systems do have a built-in CMI component. However, in many microcomputer-based systems or recent years this is quite rudimentary, restricted perhaps to the scoring of a student's success on the questions in a given lesson and summarizing this in a final report. As soon as the student switches the computer off, these data may be lost. Other micro-based systems are a little more sophisticated, in that they store these student records on the diskette, allowing more sophisticated analyses of results by the instructor/author.

Computer-based CAI systems, designed for use by large numbers of students at distributed terminals, are much stronger on CMI. A good example is the PLATO Learning Management system built into Control Data's PLATO computer-based-instruction system. We shall discuss the

PLATO system in more detail later, when we analyse tutorial CAI. For the time being serves to show the wealth of data storage, organization and analysis options open to the instructor using the PLATO system. Apart from such obvious facilities as the recording and monitoring of student progress, the system offers very extensive formative evaluation possibilities geared to both the diagnosis and correction of weakness in the instructional materials design, as well as individual weaknesses and difficulties of each student. Other facilities include: control over 'who has access to what', allowing one to vary the extent of learner control over the learning process, as well as access to progress statistics; an electronic mail facility allowing individual communication between instructor and student or between students.

Stand-alone dedicated systems

A large-scale example of the second type of application was PROJECT PLAN, which was developed in the late 1960s in the USA. This project used computer-marked objective tests, to accompany all the primary and some of the secondary school curriculum in American schools. The schools subscribing to the system were equipped with special 'post office' terminals, one to a classroom. After covering a particular unit, of, say, three or four objectives, the learners, either individually or as groups, would take a pre-printed objective test, in multiple-choice format. They would respond on special cards, marking the choices by scoring the appropriate letters alongside the question's number, already pre-printed on the cards. They would also mark their individual code numbers. Then they would 'post' the cards into a slot of the terminal, to update their individual file, kept in a computer at a distance. The individual student received feedback of results and suggestions for further study. The teacher could compare the individual student's progress with that of his group and of other students and groups in other schools, right across the country. The computer was programmed to follow a highly complex control algorithm, that could use this extremely large bank of data to generate individual student profiles, individual guidance, suggestions of the best methods and materials of study for particular students or particular course objectives, predictions of success in particular types of career and so on. The system involved several thousand American school children and used an even larger database on long-term success in life, related to school performance, which had been collected in an earlier project-PROJECT TALENT-that had involved five million children.

Project PLAN used a large mainframe computer dedicated to the instructional management functions. During the life of the project, which was sponsored by the Westinghouse Corporation, schools on both sides of the USA were effectively in communication, linked through the one computer at westing-house in California. There were even some American schools as far away as Saudi Arabia, receiving on-line management services from the one computer. This may be one of the principal reasons why the project lasted only a few years. At that time-late 1960s and early 1970s - the costs of running such a service were very high, and the long distance data communication links were not all that reliable. Neither of these limitations are true today and, although project PLAN is no longer with us, many similar large-scale CMI systems are currently operating in various countries. Perhaps one of the biggest is the system operated by the US Navy. However, the British Open University operates a somewhat more limited sort of CMI capability. Other open learning systems are following suit, the Open University of China for example, with over one million students, would have difficulty in achieving effective instructional management without extensive computer assistance.

Stand-alone time-sharing systems

However, stand-alone CMI system do not have to be so big, not do they need a dedicated computer system. Some of the earliest systematic research and development on computers in education used a little bit of spare time in an existing multipurpose computer to manage classroom-based or print-based programmed instructional systems. At the University of Aston in Birmingham, U.K. Croxton and Martin added a simple computer-based management system to an existing engineering structures course, using printed modules, and in so doing more than doubled the frequency of distinction passes on final national examinations. At the Middlesex polytechnic in London. I developed a CMI system to accompany a remedial mathematics course offered to fresh man undergraduates in social sciences as a totally individualized programmed instruction unit of 20 modules. The tutor would would only be involved in the teaching role with those students and on those modules where the self-instructional materials had proved to be inadequate.

The traditional 'system-control' model of CMI

This model is seen to assume-0three general characteristics for the course that is being managed. These are:

1. *Individualization.* The instruction is assumed to be individualized to a greater or lesser extent, in terms of learning rate, methods, media, even content and objectives in some cases.
2. *Behavioural objectives.* The instruction is assumed to be designed on the basis of a task analysis that established a set of specific behavioural objectives.
3. *Educational technology principles.* The instruction us assumed to be designed/developed in accordance with general educational technology, principles, including some model for the selection of methods and media, some model for the measurement and control of mastery of the pre-specified objectives, and so on.

A Learner-control model of CMI

These three assumptions are generally apparent in the majority of CMI systems developed to date. However, in recent years, with the development of database management technology, there is a new trend that may prove very important. This is the trend towards the structuring of bodies of knowledge in the form of so called 'knowledge bases'. Such knowledge bases are essential components of the new 'AI' generation of problem-solving software but they may also be used as resources by learners to identify the knowledge required for a purpose of the learner's own choosing. The management system of such a knowledge base is not centred on specific behavioural objectives, but must identify and present the knowledge content relevant to some personal objective that the learner brings to the exercise, which may not be fully predictable in advance. Such knowledge-base management systems may be important elements in CMI systems of the future. An example of such a system is embedded in a digital-electronics course. I helped to develop for the rapid and flexible retraining/updating of electronics technicians. This is basically a laboratory/workshop-based course, organized in a series of two-week modules. The instructor spends most of his or her time on the practical laboratory/workshop exercises. The underlying electronics, mathematics and logic theory is available in a large number of reference sheets which are organized in the form of a knowledge base. This is intended to include all the knowledge that an electronics technician working with digital logic circuits may require, whatever the specific industry/application/state of sophistication of the technology, etc. Anyone entering the course should be able to locate, quickly and completely, all the information relevant to current activity in the laboratory, be presented with specific relevant example, at an appropriate level of difficulty, and receive appropriate self-testing questions and exercises. This completely random-access system of information presentation is managed by a simple database applications package.

Computer-assisted testing

Computer-based test-item banks

Computer-based testing may be part of a CAI system, or may be a stand-alone facility. Some computer-based testing facilities are no more than an item bank, which can be used to generate two or more tests of equivalent content and difficulty, to be used at different moments in conventional classroom teaching/testing. Such systems are no more than a specialist application of databases-each test item is classified according to several parameters. The instructor may request the print-out of a test of X items, of Y difficulty level, with Z content-type on a given set of objectives. The item bank contains a sufficient number of test items in each of these categories to enable random selection of items to generate several quite different test-papers which are, however, equivalent. Such an application is stand-alone, does not require the student to interact with the computer and does not score the test or analyse the results. As it stands, such an application would not be considered by anyone as an example of computer-assisted-instruction. It is 'computer-assisted-test construction'.

Computer-based on line testing

When, however, the student takes the test on-line at a computer terminal, when the test is automatically scored and the results analysed, and when that analysis results in some final guidance message to the student then we have a level of assistance in testing that takes on part of the instructional function. For example, in the case of the 20-module remedial maths course mentioned earlier, early versions of the CMI system were based on a 20-part diagnostic paper-based test, that all students took on entry.

This was scored by a monitor who then entered the test results into the computer for analysis, prescription of an individual study plan and control of student progress. In later versions, however, the students would take the diagnostic test on-line. This offered one immediate benefit. In the earlier system, a weak student would spend a lot of time getting all the items of the massive diagnostic test wrong. When taken no-line, the computer keeps track of student performance as he or she takes the test and, as soon as error rates on a given section of the test exceed acceptable limits, the testing stops, a partial prescription is given and the student goes off to pick up the module in the resource centre. After studying, the student returns to the computer terminal, automatically picks up the test at the point where he or she had difficulties, gets post-tested on the skills just studied hopefully succeeds this time and proceeds further into the diagnostic system until another weakness is identified and the appropriate study module is prescribed. In this set-up, the diagnostic pre-testing and post-testing are completely administered and managed by the computer. These are, of course, essential components of the instructional system, so we can look on this computer-assisted testing procedure as a form of partial CAI. It would only require the study material to be converted into computer-based information screens, to transform the whole system into a CAI tutorial.

Drill and practice

Early research at standford university

Some of the earliest research an development related to drill ad practice exercises on computers was performed by Patrick Suppes and his collaborators at Standford University in the 1960s. The major findings of these studies supported the thesis that, at least in the area of mathematical skills, well designed drill and practice routines could develop higher levels of competence, in less time than was normally the case when other means of organizing the practice sessions were tried.

Since those early days, the number of different draft applications has increased and, of course, the costs of computers and software development have fallen, turning Suppes' effective, but exceedingly expensive, techniques into everyday reality. The type of sophisticated, matrix-based, model of complexity and difficulty in a given set of problems, may be quite easily accommodated in even quite a modest computer. As a guide, the memory needed to run the type of complex drill and practice routines designed by Suppes is much less than that required to run a reasonably sophisticated version of VISICALC, SUPERCALC or one of the other spreadsheet programmes now available for most home computers in the 32K RAM or upwards range of memory.

The basic organization of a set of practice maths problems in a given skill domain. The practice items are classified according to complexity and difficulty. Depending on success in correct solution of examples at a given point of complexity and difficulty, students will progress to more challenging examples, or get more practice at lower levels.

The real importance of drill and practice

This mode is unduly criticized by some people, as being a 'lesser from' of CAI. We would not agree. There are, of course, whole areas of the curriculum and whole classes of objectives, for which this mode of practice is not appropriate. However, there are also whole areas where some form of drilling is necessary in order to develop basic skills or to reinforce essential knowledge. No one learns a foreign vocabulary without the need to practice and repeat the words. This may occur in the natural context of using the language. But if one is in a hurry, some artificial drilling exercise is needed. If the computer can offer entertaining and efficient drill exercises at an economic cost, there is nothing 'second class' about it. If a clerk has to develop a high level of skill in the performance of a routine task, such as the error-free calculation of pay-as-you-earn tax deductions from employees' wage packets and a computer based drill proves to be the most effective and efficient means of developing this skill, why should we frown on this form of application?

We are rather of the opinion that drill ad practice, though not very spectacular, is destined to be one of the main uses of CAI, as long as people have to learn routine and repetitive tasks of any nature.

Drill and practice 'shells'-prepare your own exercises

A number of versatile packages, rather like the test packages described earlier, are now available, that allow the teacher to change the content of the exercise while maintaining the general format of the exercise. The difference between these drill exercises and the test packages mentioned earlier, is in the form of feedback supplied to the student and in the conscious effort to develop the mastery of specific objectives. Once again, many of these exercises are disguised as games and are often, indeed, based on well known games, adapted to the computer based format. Some of these, marketed by Wida Software, are specifically designed to develop associations, as in the learning of a new vocabulary. One version is an adaptation of the card game, of SNAP. Two words or phrases appear on the screen at any one time, one in each language. The words change in a random fashion, first one then the other. At times the two words which are visible are equivalent-in that case, the player must register that he/she observed the association, by depressing a key. If the key is not depressed within a certain time limit, the computer gains a point. If the player responds within the time limit, he/she gains a point. There are nine different speeds of play that can be pre-set at the beginning of the exercise. The game can be used for any association-learning, where rapid identification response is an asset; e.g. in understanding a foreign spoken conversation, in learning map codes ad conventions, in identifying traffic signs and in many other association and discrimination learning situations.

Odd man out

Another exercise, named *odd man out* presents four words or short phrases on the screen, three of which belong to one class and one belongs to another. The player must identify the odd man out, by keying in the appropriate code number. If correct, the player obtains confirmative feedback, together with an explanation of the classifying concept used. If incorrect, the player receives corrective feedback and, once again, an explanation of the basis for the classification. In this, way, a whole range of concepts can be drilled to perfection. One application would be in the recognition and classification of parts of speech. The game would be 'loaded' with four adjective,s four verbs, four adverbs, four prepositions and son on. The computer then selects, randomly, three examples from one group and one from another. Other applications for which we have used this format of drill include the training of supermarket checkout staff in the classification of products sold according to stock-control categories, the training of postmen to classify streets according to postal delivery rounds, the drilling of 'town and river' type of factual information in geography and the classification of animals and plants in biology. It is a drill format that is suitable for the development of most concepts, especially groups of interrelated and easily confused concepts.

Jackpot

Yet another drill game, supplied by Wida Software, is based on the simulation, on the computer screen, of a 'one-armed bandit' fruit machine. Three cylinders can be rotated, by pressing appropriate keys. Imaginary 'coins' have to be fed to the computer to make it play. At certain, randomly occurring moments in the game, the player gains the right to hold or to 'nudge' one or more of the cylinders, just as in the real-life gambling machines. However, instead of attempting to line up three lemons, or other winning combinations of fruit, the player must line up three works that, together, 'make sense'. Once again, the content of the drill may be changed at will. The game was originally designed to drill correct sentence formation in foreign language teaching. However, with a bit of ingenuity, other applications may be invented. One history application involved the matching of *who* did *what* and *when*.

Drill and practice of manual skills on simulators

However, simulators, based on computers, have many applications in the drill and practice mode. A classic and very illuminating example is Gordon Pask's SAKI, developed in the early 1960s, but only recently generally available, due to the fall of computer prices. The SAKI machine was initially devised to train the skills of punching a numerical keypad of ten digits. A later, more sophisticated version was developed to train and drill typing skills. The trainee is presented with a keyboard that has no markings on the keys and two screens. One screen presents information to be typed and the other shows a picture of the keyboard layout on which the keys light up to indicate the position of the key to be pressed at a given moment. The trainee approaches the simulator after some initial instruction on correct technique, typing rhythm and related essential knowledge.

Randomly selected letters appear on screen 1 and the position of each appropriate key is 'cued' by the lights that appear on the simulated keyboard on screen 2. As practice progress the general speed of presentation of data to be typed increases, and the intensity of the lights not he simulated keyboard decreases. However, all this happens in function of the error pattern and response rate of the trainee. He/she gets longer to respond to the letters which give difficulty, gets more intense cues and over longer period of time for these letters and, furthermore, these letters begin to occur at a frequency proportional to their level of difficulty. All this occurs in response to a particular trainee's individual pattern of errors. He/she gets more practice more time to respond and more help, adjusted on a continuous, 'on-line' basis by the control algorithm built into the trainer. This highly adaptive learning environment is extremely efficient, leading typical learners to achieve first-rate typing speeds in only a few hours of drill and practice.

Similar adaptive, computer-based, training devices now are fairly common for developing psychomotor and perceptual skills, such as radar tracking, missile firing and aircraft gunnery. Many arcade and home video games also develop, perhaps not all that intentionally, certain basic coordination or manipulation skills. It is more difficult to classify such devices as the full scale flight simulators, or Moore's 'talking typewriter' used for the automated teaching of writing and reading skills. Basically, they too are simulated environments that provide the opportunity for intensive practice of some basic skills. However, a lot of initial learning may also take place during the experience.

An illustrative example of this category, which contrasts with the SAKI system, is the EASY LEARN keyboard training station, initially developed for the British Post Office and now marketed by Hi-

Port Systems in the United Kingdom. This is a full-function keyboard trainer, that can be used as a stand-alone individual trainer, or linked in groups to an instructor terminal for use as a form of learning laboratory. Only one screen is used and this can be used to present a variety of displays, including stimulus material to be copy-typed by the trainee and explanatory presentations, to teach the basic rules of efficient keyboard technique. It is some of the variety of presentations that the trainee receives at different stages of the programme. The system may be used in the 'conditional' mode in which trainees only progress to new material after a correct response and correction of any errors, or in the 'unconditional' mode which allows progress irrespective of errors.

The 'programmed tutorial mode of CAI

The programmed tutorial mode of CAI is indeed akin to 'computer-based programmed instruction'. All the most commonly used techniques of the early days of programmed instruction are now being revived and applied in the design of CAI programmed tutorial sequences. Both linear and branching structures are used, through many people argue that the use of a computer to present a linear instructional sequence is rather like using a steam-hammer to crack a nut. This may, in general, be true, though there are some instances in which computer generated effects or the computer control of ancillary media or equipment, may justify the application.

The possibilities for creative use of branching

In relation of branching, the computer opens up a range of possibilities that would have been difficult to arrange in the scrambled text, or primitive teaching machine, days of the 1060s. Theoretically, the computer can be programmed to branch to any number of alternatives, not to a limit of four or five at most, restricted by the number of plausible choices that the instructional designer can invent for one given multiple choice' question, and also by the difficult of organizing the pages in a scrambled text when there are very many different routes through the book.

In theory, a large library of computer-based instructional materials could be cross-referenced and indexed in a way that permitted students to back-track to a new context but has unfortunately been forgotten through lack of use. Branching decisions, to faster or slower streams of instructional presentation, can be taken on the basis of a cumulative analysis of several responses over time and not just on the last, possibly atypical, response made. A variety of other non-computer-based materials may be incorporated into the system, their use being prescribed by the diagnoses of individual student progress and needs, that are constantly being prepared and updated by the computer. These alternative materials may be visual, as in videodise and interactive videocassette systems already on the market. They may be print-based reading assignments, annotated bibliographies for free study, laboratory or workshop-based experiments and practical exercises, or specific group-learning activities. They may be all of these, knitted into a complex, multi-media, computer-controlled, truly individualized instructional system.

The reality is not always that creative

Unfortunately, in practice, few real CAI systems exploit these possibilities to the full. Too many are totally computer-based when they could be more effective and more economical if they were partly based on other media. Too many are a mixture of linear and branching sequences, not very different from programmes that actually existed in print and paper form some 20 years ago. Too many are not even good examples of ostensibly CAI systems that did not really different much from a standard textbook-presented electronically. They did not even follow the three basic principles of instructional programming:

- Active participation, by learners, in the learning process.
- Immediate knowledge of results and corrective feedback.
- Avoidance of excessive errors on the part of the learners. Still less did they show creativity and perspicacity in the analysis of typical students' errors and difficulties, and the design of appropriate instructional solutions.

For want of a better starting point, the basic principles and techniques of programmed instruction, which have stood the test of time should be systematically and creativity applied in the design of programmed tutorial CAI.

However, if one merely applies the basic techniques of programmed instruction, it is often difficult to justify the use of a computer to present the material. The figure presents the original version of a step in a CAI sequence on set theory. This step introduces the concept of 'UNION'. It is reasonably well designed in that it supplements the formal definition by an example. Then the exercise that follows tests comprehension of the concept, by application to a specific case. It would have been better, though, to ask students to generate a response rather than merely selecting one from a set of suggestion. This is the difference between construction and recognition of an appropriate response. However, the author seems to have been so conditioned by the multiple-choice single-letter response format that was required by early teaching machines and most scrambled text' branching programmed, that he/she has overlooked that in a computer-based application we can ask the student to construct a response ad then write a routine to analyse and classify and response in relation to its source of error, thus matching it to an appropriate feedback comment.

The modification in the method of asking for a response, introduced, is the least that could be done in order to make use of the capabilities that computers offer over and above those present in textual presentation. By we can do more. The feedback comments in the two versions illustrate another point. In the original version, the feedback is very categorical and the corrective strategy is to suggest re-reading the present screen of information and try to answer again. This is a further legacy of print-based self instruction. Any more complex branching would lead to excessive page turning and any benefit from enrichment of the branching might be outweighed by lost time looking for correct page ad the possibility of losing one's place together. When presented by computer, however, any amount of to and fro branching can be handled quickly and smoothly. As the error illustrated may be a mere slip on the part of the student, or may have deeper causes, why not plan for alternative alternative forms of corrective feedback. We can allow for the student who immediately sees his error when presented with the feedback message and for the student who found the bare formal definition insufficiently clear and would like more and more practical examples to improve his understanding of the new concept. We can allow for the very unsure student, who would like to back track to the earlier concept that he has confused with the new one. We have left these options under student control, but we could bring these alternatives under programme control, by asking subsidiary questions which would help to diagnose the seriousness and source of the individual student's misconception.

Another possible enhancement that would be easy to introduce would be the substitution of a different practice example of equivalent difficulty for each subsequent wrong answer so that students do not have the chance to zero in one the correct answer by a process of trial and error. One could, of course, use many other computer-based tricks, like animating the Venn diagrams and showing the union of two sets forming a new set with all the elements included in one circle. Whether this would enhance learning, or would just be a gimmicky application of the 'bells and whistles', is a moot point. Finally, of course, we could abandon the basic original tutorial design and opt for a discovery-learning conversational strategy, or a simulation perhaps-if we can justify it.

Conversational or dialogue tutorial CAI

'Intelligent' CAI

There are many different approaches that may be classified in this category of CAI. Some are referred to as 'Socratic' dialogue and are based on a mixed-initiative strategy, where both computer and student may either ask or respond to questions. Such tutorials are based on 'artificial intelligence' models of the teaching learning process and require very complicated and time consuming programming in little used and difficult to learn programming languages, such as Lisp or Prolog. It is not surprising, therefore that, at the time of writing most of these systems are research laboratory playthings, rather than widely used and practically cost-effective instructional systems. They include such early systems as SCHOLAR and CASTE and more recent ones such as SOPHIE. They differ very much from each other in terms of the specific models for interaction and learning/teaching upon which they operate. But they have the common element of adaptiveness to the individual learner by some means of 'learning about the learner'. This is where they attempt to model the expert human tutor more closely than other forms of CAI and, therefore, they have gained the popular name of 'intelligent tutoring systems' or more coloquially 'Intelligent Computer Assisted Instruction'.

However, not all conversational, in-dept dialogue, CAI methodologies are based on the concept of the computer learning about the learner and thus improving and further individualizing the instructional strategy being used. It is possible to build some very complex interactive dialogues purely on the basis of deep questioning techniques and multi-faceted analyses of the responses given by the student. After all, this is what happens in many university courses as the general rule, especially when student/staff ratios are high. The professor teaching a large group seldom gets to know all the students.

However, by setting suitably deep and multi-faceted 'essay' or 'seminar' type assignments the professor can get a very accurate picture of the individual student's present conceptual schema on a given topic. In his or her reply to the essay or the seminar presentation, the professor can be very perceptive and helpful to the individual although the only data available to the professor is the content of a complex written or spoken argument on the topic, prepared by the specific student in question, together with accumulated experience of how students in general react to the topic, what difficulties or misconceptions they have, etc. One very successful approach to the simulation of such professor student interchanges on specific complex problems on a computer is the technique fall Structural Communication, developed by Hodgson and his associates in the United Kingdom at the end of the 1960s. This method is based on the analysis of a multi-faceted multiple choice response which the student constructs by selection of a combination of response components from a 20 to 40 item 'response matrix' . The construction of such in-depth, interactive tutorial dialogues is quite complex from the viewpoint of subject matter expertise and knowledge structure analysis, but relatively simple in terms of the computer hardware and software required.

Computer-based simulation

Whereas the conversational,or dialogue, modes of CAI are perhaps among the least practised on a large scale, SIMULATION is probably the most used and fastest growing mode. This is probably due to a series of factors.

Why use simulations?

- Computer-based simulations are sometimes the only way of developing certain types of learning experiences.
- They use the particular advantage of the computer as an ultra-rapid calculating and data processing machine, to the best advantage.
- The computer may often play a part in a more

elaborate, not entirely computer-based simulation-game.

- Unlike the conversation mode, simulations are often quite simple to plan form the instructional viewpoint. Thus, the instructional designer may delegate a major part of the production task to specialist computer staff.
- The use of simulations is usually an adjunct to normal teaching procedures-it does not disrupt traditional organizational practices, upset conventional teachers by threatening the jobs of anyone, or tie up the computer on a nearly permanent basic for instruction.
- Many computer-based simulations are in the science area, where staff are most receptive to the new technology.
- There are, however, ample valid applications for this mode in almost any educational or training context.

The applications abound. One area in which dozens, perhaps hundreds of successful simulations have been developed, medical education. Trainee doctors learn how patients with diabetes react to the intake of sugar in various quantities. Other simulations teach abut the reactions of the body to different drugs or medicines. Yet others deal with environmental factors that promote epidemics,. the control of a common disease by the vaccination of different proportions of the population. In all such simulations, the student may vary some of the critical variables and observe how other variables are affected.

Another popular area for process simulations is in the sciences. Ellington, Addinall and Percival list dozens of examples, including a simulation f process-of discharge of a capacitor, the flow of fluids through nozzles, gaseous diffusion, gravitation, interference and diffraction patterns of light waves, motion of satellites in orbits, and many others.

Complex multifaceted simulations

There is one other application to be mentioned here-the flight simulator. Simple navigational simulators one down the road, for operation on most makes of home are a form of *decision-making exercise.* They teach more or less accurately, the factors that must be taken into account when flying and navigating a plane. In playing with these simulators, one learns when to drop the undercarriage, in relation to air speed, when and how much to trim the flaps, how to allow for a cross wind when approaching an airfield, and so on. Such a software package, sold as a game for recreational purposes, does therefore give practice in the decision-making aspects of flying. At it presents the player with up to three visual displays-the instrument panel, the view in front of the cockpit and a map of the area on which the plane is situated-it is a simulation of the navigational and instrument-flying tasks in the pilot's job. When this same decision-making package is incorporated in a model of a real plane, that also supplies the correct physical feel, guidance and feedback for the manual skills of control, we have introduced the element of *apparatus operation.*

Database Inquiry

The final classification in our schema of CAI only just qualities to be included as a category of 'institution': it is really a mode of *information retrieval* from some form of organized bank of information, or *database*. However, if the database is organized to supply all the information necessary to achieve certain groups of educational objectives and if the learner is given a set of specific objectives to be achieved, then we have a form of instructional system indeed, a very flexible self-instructional system.

The instructional and the 'Serendipity' Use of a Database

There is, on the other hand, the unstructured, 'browsing' use of a computerized database, analogous to browsing in a public library, which is not aimed towards specific learning objectives and is therefore not 'instruction in the sense that we are using the term. This is what Nicholas Rsushby termed 'serendipity learning'. The planning of a bank of information for unstructured, serendipity learning, is not unlike the planning of the purchasing policy of a public library. We do not know exactly who will turn up to use the resources, or what they will be looking for. We do, however, have some information concerning the demand, by analysis of the request we receive, through study of the bestseller lists, by careful analysis of the reports on new publications, and so on. how well we satisfy demand can be assessed through the study of user reactions, rather than the measurement of specific objectives achieved.

The 'global library'

One potential growth area for the application of the computer in education is, no doubt, the creation of computer-based libraries, computer-based information banks on specific subjects, etc. One such application already in use in UK is Prestel. Other videotext systems, available to the public in general and devoted to educational and cultural purposes, as opposed to advertising and newcasting, will no doubt appear in increasing numbers, throughout the world. Pundits already draw mental images of immense national or even international networks linking dozens of specialist libraries into one huge system which, to use the works or Roy Jenkins, 'can allow the contents of all the world's great libraries to flow through every living room in the land'.

The organization of information for retrieval

This vision, to become a functioning reality, will need a lot of work on the organization of the information of these 'great libraries' in such a manner that the not-too-skilled potential user can find his way about, locate what he wants, or what he might want if he only knew that it existed. The task of organizing such immense databases is not all that well understood. Many people are now interested in the topic and much research is under way. In relation to educational, scientific and other specialist use of such systems, the need is felt for a technology of subject matter analysis and organization that can produce a database on a given subject that is as helpful to the learner/researcher, as a human expert on the subject would be, if available for a personal interview. This has led to the concept of Expert Systems-computer-based information banks which emulate a human expert in a given subject area.

Expert systems

a database on a specialist subject is, however, little more than a well organized and cross-referenced library. It is an important and useful tool in the hands of an expert. However, it does not take over the role of the expert. The important aspect of a true expert system is that it takes on at least part of the problem-organization and problem-solving roles on the human expert. It is capable not only furnishing the information solicited, but should be able to interrogate the user for relevant input information, prompt the user in the steps to be followed in solving a problem, or even take over the problem-solving process as a whole.

The special-purpose scientific software that solves a set of pre-determined equations has been with us for a long time any computer programme is a 'problem solver' in this sense. But the solution of complex problems that require one to weigh various factors in relation to each other and make a decision on incomplete data-that is, *heuristic* problem solving-has only recently been successfully computerized. The 'expert system' is one form of a computerized heuristic problem solver.

Learning through programming

Taylor's classification of the computer in education as 'Tutor, Tool and Tutee' emphasizes that one major way in which computes are used by learners is to learn how to programme them. The computer is Tutee, in the sense that it is the learner who takes on the role of 'tutor' or rather, programmer. There are two justifications for such as an approach, one related to the development of specific programming skills, the other related to the development of general problem-solving skills and 'powerful ideas'.

Vocational and non-vocational reasons for learning to programme

The argument that learning to programme the computer is best achieved through practice in programming the computer is unassailable. However, who needs computer programming skills? Well, those who earn their livelihood by programming computers. But the idea, born with the appearance of cheap microcomputers, that all computer users would engage in some programming, is last dying. The 'vocational training' argument for teaching computing to every one is not strong, and we can see how recently the concept of 'computer literacy' and been changing-whereas in the early 1980s just about all such programmes in included instruction in one or more computer languages, the late 1980s tendency is towards much less emphasis on programming languages and much more on the efficient use of special purpose applications software.

This trend is spurred on by expediency-by the need to concentrate on what is immediately useful. But there are many educators and computer scientists who argue that a knowledge of computing has general value as a discipline in logical thinking, problem formulation and solution, etc. They argue that experience in programming is time well spent in any student's general education, whatever their future vocational needs might turn out to be. Not all educators agree. Some remember that for centuries the inclusion of Latin as an obligatory subject in the general school curriculum was defended largely on the grounds that 'Latin in a logical language and therefore, through learning Latin, students would learn to think logically'. There was no shred of evidence to suggest that this was in fact so, but the pressure group for Latin was so strong that many generations of argument were needed in order to introduce a change in the curriculum. Are we witnessing a similar 'pressure group' situation developing in respect of computer studies in the general curriculum? Or is there some real evidence that learning to programme has some more general educational effects?

The answer from the 'pressure group' is that of course it depends on what language you learn and on how it is taught. The majority of computer scientists criticize the inclusion of BASIC as an introductory computing experience, arguing that the structure of this language is not conductive to the learning of good programming strategies. The educators, on the other hand, argue that the programming experience should be planned to include concepts of more general utility. The juxtaposition of these two opinions largely explains the popularity of LOGO, since its appearance in microcomputer versions in the early 1980s. Before we look at the evidence, let us examine just what LOGO is and how it is being used in schools.

LOGO - Its origins

LOGO was developed at Massachusetts Institute of Technology, by a team of educators and computer scientists interested in logic programming and Piagetian concepts of child development. This, at first sight, rather strange combination of interests came about when Seymour Papert, a student of Praget and interested in implementing his ideas in education, joined the faculty of MIT, at that time on the leading research centres on artificial intelligence. The current 'AI' programming language LISP, a powerful but not too easy to learn tool. The MIT team was working on, the development of a simpler version.. Papert saw, in this development, the opportunity to introduce young children to logic programming at a very early age and through this, to create a computer-based 'learning environment in which children could discover for themselves most of the concepts and relationships of mathematics. Papert's ideas stimulated a lot of excitement in the 'AT fraternity and led to a number of projects in the mid 1070s. Notable among these was the Brookline LOGO project. Projects like these were exploratory 'let's see what can be done' studies, rather than strict research. The Edinburgh project was perhaps the more rigorous in that standard mathematics tests were administered to students participating in the project. However, these projects served more to illustrate the potential for creative use of computers with young children, rather than any spectacular learning improvement towards the accepted school mathematics objectives. The experience gained in these projects, was synthesized in Papert's classic book Mindstroms which appeared at the same time that microcomputer versions of LOGO were released on the market. Thus the LOGO movement was lunched.

The geometry and recursion

One aspect that Papert built into LOGO was the 'Turtle', triangular cursor that can be moved and rotated by the user, to create a geometrical drawing. How a child can build a simple shape by writing a short programme and the use that shape as a component t build much more complex figures. The capacity of LOGO to allow the user to define his own commands and thus extend the power of the language, is one of its main attractions and strengths. The programmer uses the idea of 'recursion' to simplify the structure of the programme. Recursion means 'repeat what you already know, well illustrated in the

'SPOINSQUARE' programme. The complex figure is drawn by using the previously defined command and repeating several times with small changes in size and rotation. By experimenting with such programming. Papert argues, children gain insights into how complex ideas are structured from simpler ones. This insight, gained in the context of 'turtle geometry', is claimed to transfer to other domains of learning as well.

We shall examine later on some of the research on whether the claims made for using LOGO really do stand up. There is no doubt that the introduction of LOGO in schools has contributed much to the de-mystification of computers and has created some very entertaining educational activities. What is not so clear is whether any world-shaking change in learning has taken place.

Research on the use of computer for learning

Comparative studies: computers vs. teachers

Meta-analyses of studies on CAL

In earlier chapters we reviewed the studies comparing the use of a given medium with so-called 'conventional instruction'. In all cases, we found that very many such studies have been carried out, but he results are, to say the least, inconclusive. With some notable exceptions, well designed comparative research has shown, at best, a slight improvement in learning for the mediated version of the lessons compared. More often, analysis has shown 'no significant difference'. We have seen that a more sophisticated approach to the analysis of the data from many similar studies has been tried by Kulik and his collaborators. Not surprisingly, Kulik has performed a series of such 'meta analysis' studies on the very large number of comparative studies on CAL-one analysis of comparison studies in higher education and one in elementary education. All there of these 'meta-analyses' involving the combination of hundreds of separate comparative research studies, showed significant, if not spectacularly large, advantages for the computer-based materials, over the teacher administered lessons.

Possible limitations of comparative research and Clark's position on effect of media on instruction

These meta analyses have come under fire from several writes. Some have argued that many comparative studies may induce the teachers involved to take extra pains over their lesson planning and delivery as they find themselves 'on trial' and thus the CAL benefits normally attainable would be reduced or masked. Others argue that the opposite effect may be present-the extra effort, time and instructional design skill that has gone into the development of the computer-based materials results in superior lesson designs and exaggerate the effect of the computer. Clark indeed re-analysed the results of the Kulik studies, discarding the poorly designed studies and separating those in which the same teacher was responsible for the development of the CAL material and for the conventional class teaching, from those where different teachers taught the control classes. He found that when the same teacher was both author of the CAL materials and instructor of the classroom-based control group, the advantage for the computer-based instruction was much reduced. He argues that, probably, this is because in those studies there is more similarity in the basic instructional design of the two alternatives being compared and, if this similarity were to be controlled rigorously in all studies, there would probably be no significant advantage of the computer administered lessons over the teacher-delivered instruction. He concludes by arguing that, as was the case with his findings in the case of video and other mediated instruction, computers make no more contribution to learning than the truck which delivers groceries to the market contributes to improved nutrition in a community. Purchasing a truck will not improve nutrition just as purchasing a computer will not improve student achievement. Nutrition gains come from getting the correct groceries to the people who need them. Similarly, achievement gains result from matching the correct teaching method to the student who needs it.'

Implications for CAL research

Now, this apparent criticism of CAL is really no more than a criticism of the comparative studies that form such a large percentage of the research. When all possible variables have been controlled and balanced, it is not at all surprising to find no difference between any two presentation media. However, this implies that the content of learning selected for a comparative study must be such that it is equally capable of being presented by the various media being compared. It also implies that the teaching methods implemented in a study must be capable of being implemented equally well in all the media being compared. And there is ample evidence to suggest that the really effective way of using computers in teaching is to implement by the unaided classroom teacher. One use of CAL which is so defended is the computer-based simulation/games, in that it presents real life-like experience to all students within realistic time-frames, in a way that was hitherto impossible. Another argument is that many instructional designs that could, in theory, be implemented by the unaided teacher do not generally get to be implemented because they are too time consuming or difficult to use on a day-to-day basis, But the high speed of data processing offered by the computer makes these designs practically viable (examples include sophisticated drill and practice designs which require the detailed tracking of the performance of each student in order to select the most appropriate practice examples-see the examples of maths drills and typing discussed above).

So, to find the real benefits of the use of computers as instruments of instruction, we should look for real problems that have been solved, or real improvements that have been gained by the use of CAL. These 'case studies' may turn out to be more informative than formal research studies. They are capable of showing the effect of a number of the medium's characteristics over a significant period of time. They may also suggest benefits which are not measured by the standard testing procedures of formal research.

CMI in Formal Education

Such case studies abound in just about all the categories of CAL that were described in the previous section. To start with computer-managed instruction, one should note the many reported success stories that document the benefit actually achieved when previously existing non-CAI courses were enhanced with an element of computer-based management. The case of the Engineering Structure course at the University of Aston in the UK, mentioned earlier, is a notable example in this category. By adding a computer-managed diagnosis system to an existing, self-study module-based, university level course, the authors succeeded in raising the success rates of their students on nationally administered examinations to such an extent that *all* their students' results fell in the top 10 per cent of the national score distribution. This result was so outstanding, in relation to that particular university's previous record and in terms of the students' outstanding results in structures but not necessarily in any of the other engineering examinations, that the examining body initially refused to believe that some form of 'cheating' was not involved. Only after the students took a second 'cheatproofed' structures exam and achieved similar outstanding results, did the new teaching method get the credit that was due to it.

Why CMI makes a difference

The main reason for the spectacular improvement was in fact nothing more than the increased level of diagnostic control that could be exerted when the computer was used to process the results of the week-by-week study assignments. With 300 or more students registered on a lecture-and-modules based course, there was no way for faculty to keep track of individual progress until it was too late to do anything about individual learning problems. With rapid computer-based diagnosis of learning progress, it was possible to use all existing teaching resources to give the maximum of individual coaching (not-much, with the staff-student ratio available, but the little possible made all the difference).

Efficiency of on-line testing

The use of computer-assisted testing also has its share of success stories. One, already described earlier, was the added smoothness and practically that on-line diagnostic testing introduced into a remedial mathematics 'learning-by-appointment' system that had been running previously on the basis of paper tests. Other benefits of the on-line 'adaptive' testing approach are documented by Weiss who shows that to achieve similar levels of precision in diagnosis, computer-based adaptive tests use 30-50 per cent fewer test questions than a similar paper-and-pencil test. This saves testing time, cuts down on student effort and reduces the frustration of the weaker student faced with many over-difficult questions to tackle and knowing that he/she will almost certainly answer incorrectly.

Utility of test-item banks

A further form of benefit that has often been gained in practice is increased facility in the construction of appropriate levels of tests and, therefore, increased use of systematic diagnostic testing procedures. This benefit comes about through the mere existence of a test item bank on a given subject matter, organized according to objective, difficulty level, et. Such an item bank may be constructed by small contributions from many teachers and is then available to all teachers as a service. Lippey describes how such computer-assisted testing may be used and gives examples of then benefits achieved.

Uses and mis-uses of drill and practice and case studies of keyboard skills drill and practice

The drill and practice mode of CAI has often been attacked as an uncreative and anti-educational use of the computer. But really, this criticism should be levelled not at the medium but at the method. WHEN USED INAPPROPRIATELY. To be sure, kids are often drilled into memorizing useless information or into executing useful procedures without real understanding of what they are learning. But there are also quite valid for drills in both education and training. The learning of foreign language vocabularies is one examples where repeated use is essential and some form of drill exercises, whether computer base or not, are appropriate. High-speed reflex skills, like typing and computer keyboard operation, are another outstanding example of a type of learning which is heavily dependent on drill and practice and where computer-based drills have shown themselves to be vastly superior to any previous training method. We mentioned in previous sections of this chapter, the early SAKI keyboard trainer and the later *easylearn* system developed for the British post office. These systems have shown themselves to be most effective, achieving results that were unknown under conventional classroom instruction. 'Twice the typing speed in half the learning time, or your money back,' are slogans that can safely be used in marketing these systems, as practical experience has shown that such results are nearly always achieved by motivated learners.

Limitations of computers as Presentation Media

Coming now to TUTORIAL CAI, we should remember that all the previously mentioned modes are often, and indeed should almost always, be present in tutorial. Individual student progress is monitored and managed by the changing of the path through the materials in response to individual needs. This necessarily involves computer-based testing which is adaptive in nature. When drills are appropriate, they may be built in and may also be made more palatable by the use of game-like contexts for practice. The extra characteristic of the tutorial is the presentation of new information to be learnt. This may be more or less effective than it would have been by means of other media. Until recently, for example, there were serious limitations on the degree of resolution of the graphic materials that could be presented on most school-use microcomputers. This aspect has improved significantly as more powerful graphics packages have become available. Also the current trend towards the linking of CAI tutorials with video material from laser dises has effectively overcome the problem of visual resolution for most purposes. But this does not make the computer screen the ideal presentation medium for all the types of information that the learner may require. The very size of the screen is sometimes a severe limitation, leading one to break down a complex network or a map, into separate screens, or to use an inconvenient 'windowing' technique in order to allow the learner to see the 'big picture'. However, for most typical instructional content, the modern computer system, enhanced with interactive video, is a pretty adequate presentation media. The benefits, if any, should be looked for in the speed and precision of storing, accessing, presenting, revising and individualizing of the information. When these are of importance, and are not achievable in the conventional teaching situation, then we can expect benefits to accure for CAI.

Benefits due to the consistency of complete CAI courses

It is for reasons such as these that there is such a discrepancy between the not-so-spectacular findings of formal comparative research studies and the reported successes of individual case studies, Kulik's meta analyses typically showed advantages to CAL over classroom instruction of the order of 15 percentage points. This is not to be 'sneezed at', if it represents a gain that can truly be expected over a long-term period, in real life instructional conditions. Clark seems to argue that the bulk of this difference is due to superior instructional design of the lesson structures given by computer and that there is no reason why similarly efficient lesson structures could not have been given in classroom instruction. But the tendency in real life classroom instruction is to have varied success with different teachers and even with different classes, taught by the same teacher. It is difficult to always maintain the same standard of teaching that was achieved during a relatively short comparative study when 'everyone was watching'. It is not surprising, therefore, that many case studies of large-scale CAI use report instructional improvements well in excess of those 15 percentage points found by Kulik.

Another benefit, reported over and over, especially in case studies of computer-based job skills training, is a significant reduction of the time required to complete a given programme of instruction. Trainees reach the required job-performance standards in an average of two-thirds or sometimes less than half the time previously required in the conventional instructional situation.

CAI segments built into classroom instruction

Of course, not all tutorial CAI is the large-scale substitution of classroom instruction by machine instruction. Much the more common situation, especially in schools, is the integration of short

CAI Tutorials on specific topics, into an overall course design, planned, implemented and partly delivered by the classroom teacher. In such a case, it is very difficult to separate out any benefits of CAI over alternative instructional designs. What can be measured is the overall effect of the teacher/computer media combination, as opposed to the teacher alone. There seems to be much less formal research along these lines. But informally, it is this sort of situation that impresses the enthusiast teacher most. The bulk of the more popular literature on the use of computers in the classroom abounds with examples of the creative integration of the computer as one of the media at the teacher's disposal. There is insufficient space in this book to explore the richness of possibilities for the integration of computer-based courseware into the conventional classroom teaching situation. Many books especially devoted to the classroom use of the computer have been written and interested reader should study some of the practical suggestions reported.

Much promise

The trend towards the development of conversational CAI was in part spurred by the limitations of the 'programmed instruction' models as a a basis for the effective use of the computer as a medium of instruction. Already in the late 1960s there were several alternative models proposed. We have already mentioned the conversational approach built into the CASTE system and the 'structural communication' approach. Both of these methods were successfully tested in paper-based tutorial versions, but the computer technology of the time was inadequate to support their use as models for the development of large-scale CAI applications. Now that the technology has caught up, we find these techniques are little used because of the great skill and effort needed to design effective materials that exploit the systems' capabilities of interaction. There are a few examples of successful implementations of conversational tutorials, but hardly any large-scale regular use.

But little progress

A similar situation exist with respect to the 'intelligent' tutorial systems that we read so much about. There is a history of research and development that spans over 30 years. Experimental systems have been operational for at last 20 years but no real impact on everyday instruction, whether in the school classroom or in job trainee situations, has as yet been felt. As Frank Roberts of Control Data remarked at the 1986 conference of the Association for the Development of Computer-assisted Instructional Systems; 'to many knowledge, some 15 or so intelligent tutorial systems have so far been developed beyond the conceptual design stage... of these, only five or six have been used at all extensively in real life instructional situations... and none have been systematically evaluated. As far as research on ICAI is concerned, we are still in the laboratory stage.

Use of simulations as components in discovery learning

The situation is very different with respect to the 'simulation' mode of CAI. This has been the fastest growing are in recent years and has the largest number of enthusiastic adherents among teachers and trainers alike. By its nature, a computer-based simulation is usually a component in a lesson. The computer is used to dynamically illustrate the cause-effect relationships that hold true in some real-life phenomenon. An example is the famous simulation of Mendel's laws in action in a computer-based fruit-fly mating experiment. In an hour or so on the computer, it is possible to simulate many generations of fruit-fly offspring for many different mating patterns. This allows students to deduce the Mendelian laws for themselves-to discover and painstaking observations. Similar discovery experience can now be conveniently arranged in just about every area of science education, as well as economics, management, etc. The educational success of such simulations is however, much dependent on how well they are introduced and followed up by the teacher. As with all experimental, or discovery, learning, it is important to reflect on the specific cases and identify the general principles at play. This is best achieved by careful initial orientation of the students and, even more importantly, deep final analysis and evaluation of what was learned. Most simulation packages do not perform these functions. The way the teacher plans and executes the briefing and debriefing is the key factor in the overall instructional effectiveness of computer-based simulations, used in the classroom for conceptual learning.

Use of simulations for learning procedures

The use of computer-based simulation to teach machine-operation is somewhat different. In this case, the instructional objectives are to learn a specific procedure. A well designed simulator may present more varied practice, more concentrated; experience of rarely occurring situations and enhanced feedback and guidance, all in a safer and possibly less environment than 'real life'.

The reports on the use of computer-based simulations tend top be generally positive. Business games, using the computer as, an interactive data bank, have been used and praised for nearly 30 years now. Computer-based simulations for procedural learning have a similarly long history, especially as embedded training for computer-related procedures but also in all branches of military training. There is a respectable body of research showing that computer-based operations training can be as effective as using the real-life equipment.

Use of simulations for higher-order learning objectives

In the cognitive learning field, the research is less conclusive. This is partly due to the points made earlier, with respect to the simulations often forming only part of the teacher's overall lesson plan. This makes it difficult to sort out whether improved learning was due to something inherent in the simulation exercise or to the skill with which the teacher exploited the experience in subsequent activities. There is a certain body of research that suggests that simulations used on their own are sometimes less effective than they appear to be. Light reports studies which show rather poor learning of factual information from business simulations that were, on the face of it, excellent and absorbing exercises. Not were concepts or principles sufficiently well generalized. There seemed to be some learning of a general 'feel' for management decision making, which was difficult to measure by normal testing methods. Oakey reported studies with situational simulation-games in which students worked in groups to solve complex problems. The objectives of the simulation-games studies included general problem-solving skills and working effectively as a group, as well as content-related objectives. He found that very little real learning had occurred, especially as related to the general problem-solving and interpersonal skills.

The benefits of 'inquiry' CAL

We are now stepping beyond what may be strictly called 'computer-assisted instruction'. A database located in a computer is an information resources. As such it may be no different in content from some other resources, say a filing cabinet or a section of a library. It is different, however, in terms of the case and speed with which specific items of information may be located. Improving the efficiency of access to information has obvious effects on the efficiency of learning. This 'tool' use of the computer thus brings automatic benefits to the instructional process, whether that process itself changes or not.

Databases used for student-directed learning

What interests us specifically in this chapter, however, is the effect of the existence of databases on the process of instruction itself. When information was difficult to access, there was a strong tendency to pre-prepare all the materials that students would use in a course of institution. These would be written up in a 'set book' or collected together as a set of 'required readings'. Students would seldom branch out beyond this prepared material. With easy access to a much wider range of resources, it is possible to design course activities around problem-statements, leaving the students responsible for the identification and selection of appropriate learning resource. This seems a natural approach at the higher level of education, as it accustoms students to do their own library research. But there is increasing evidence that it is both possible and desirable to structure instruction this way at all levels of education. Given an appropriately structured database, even elementary school children can discover for themselves, not only the facts about a subject, but also its structure and integral relationships. A database of geography facts has been found in different regions. But in searching the database for this factual information, they are led to discover the relationships that exist between climate, feeding habits, [physical attributes such as colour, size, speed, living habits such as migration and hibernation, etc. A few hours of guided searching of the database develops an understanding of a body of geography as a related whole, rather than as a set of individual facts.

Databases with expert guidance systems

It is only a small step further to develop computer-based guidance in the searching of the database, in order to create a different form of computer-assisted instruction. This approach has not received the attention that it deserves. Its potential for the promotion of student autonomy in learning is obvious. Perhaps not so obvious are the benefits of developing one package on a given subject area in such a way that many different levels of student may find it useful for many different objectives. After all, the content of the subject is comprehensively covered, if the database is to be at all useful. But the 'level of discourse' about the subject may not suit all users, unless some form of adapting this to the needs of the user were to be devised. Some may need more and simpler examples in order to understand basic concepts. Others may wish to go much deeper into practical applications of the content. Yet others may wish to engage in a philosophical analysis of the importance/implications of a given topic. A database can be structured to deal with any number of such aspects of a subject at several different levels of difficulty, so that, in theory, any user might find the information required, presented in understandable language. Of course, in order to find the appropriate content and level of discourse, the user will need help. This help function can be performed by a computer-based form of 'ex[pert guide' that is capable of interacting with any user in order to diagnose individual needs in relation to the specific databases in question. With the advent of large databases accessible from anywhere by telecommunications links, such 'intelligent' databases are beginning to generate a lot of research interest. They have even earned their own jargon name-HYPERTEXT. Like intelligent CAI, they are as yet at the stage of laboratory research, but are showing much promise.

The Benefits of LOGO

Coming now to the 'computer as tutee' as shall restrict our-selves to examining the research on the use of LOGO in education. The topic of how useful, in general educational terms, it is to learn to programme a computer is a fascinating question, but one which is not directly related to our interest here in the use of computers as instructional media. It is worth devoting a little space to the use of LOGO particularly, as so many claims have been made for its value in developing 'powerful ideas' which are generalizable to situations and content other than that used in the LOGO exercises themselves.

Lack of formal research

It should be stressed here, that LOGO if a general programming language, based on LISP and capable of being used for a variety of programming tasks. I have seen excellent examples of databases, and CAI courseware set up in LOGO. But its use in schools has generally been limited to the 'turtle geometry' aspects which are unique to this language and which were popularized so effectively by Papert and his followers. We illustrated earlier in this chapter how LOGO uses recursion, by a very simple turtle graphics programming exercises. The arguments of LOGO's supporters is that such generalizable concepts, once grasped in the context of playing with the turtle, are generalized to other branches of mathematics and indeed beyond. Para-doxically, however, there has been very little scientifically controlled research on such a theoretically interesting topic. The enthusiasts say that classical research is not appropriate, as we are witnessing highly personal learning experiences which can only adequately described by detailed case studies. The doubters argue that little research has been published because the claims made for LOGO have generally not been substantiated when research was attempted. These two viewpoints are well illustrated by one of the earliest and most intensive and controlled studies of the use of LOGO-the Edinburgh project.

Edinburgh project findings

This project involved a small group of some 11 students who attended the LOGO laboratory at Edinburgh University, regularly over a period of two years. When compared with their colleagues who had followed the same school maths studies but had not attended the LOGO experiences in the laboratory, the experimental group scored somewhat better on tests that measured comprehension of mathematical concepts, but worse on tests of mathematical procedures. The major finding reported was not measured by standardized tests, but was the observation that the experimental group were 'more willing to argue sensibly about mathematical issues' and were able to 'explain their mathematical difficulties more clearly. Other writers suggest that the benefits in mathematical reasoning reported in this and some other experiments may be due more to the attitudes and teaching methods adopted by the teachers involved than to anything intrinsic in LOGO itself.

Is LOGO Piagetian

The picture is therefore far from clear. Some teachers have, as Thronburg put it, accepted LOGO as a religion; they accepted its benefits on faith and felt that criticizing LOGO bordered on sacrilege'. Yet the widest reviews of the research literature have failed to show any very significant or systematic benefits to learning occurring from experience with LOGO. Perhaps the 'religion' syndrome is due to the Piagetian roots of Papert's philosophy. Those who believe in Piaget's view of the way that learners mature through a series of stages and progress from being 'concrete operational' learners to higher and more abstract ways of thinking, have tended to accept the LOGO approach on faith. But they forget that Piaget argues that the process is one of personal; development which cannot be hurried on by instruction. Perhaps the theoretical under pinnings of the LOGO approach are not as sound as they appeared at first sight. But perhaps the approach suffers from the incapacity of untrained teachers to get the best out of it, as Michalyuk suggest.

Deciding whether to use computer-assisted learning

'Macro' decisions; is a course suitable for CAL?

Computer-assisted learning, like other self-instructional media, can be selected as the basis of a complete, automated instructional system. Alternatively, teachers may select specific CAL, exercises as components in their overall course or lesson, deign, just as they select a set of slides on film. In the first case, the CAL, system becomes the principal medium of instruction, replacing classroom teaching entirely or at least in a large part. It implies investment in a complex system of computer-based delivers of instructional and an infrastructure of courseware development/ modification updating, hardware maintenance and repairs, etc. In the second case, the computer becomes just another instructional aid, which supplements the teacher at certain points in a course, but the teacher still remains the principal planner of each lesson and delivery medium of most parts of the lesson.

The levels of decision making

The decision of whether and the planning of how to use CAL is different in these two cases. In the first case, it is mixture of 'level I' and 'level II' considerations. On combines an analysis of overall course objectives, content, resources and constraints with overall organizational, economic and political considerations which affect the viability of the project. In the second case, when

CAL is used as a component in a lesson, its selection becomes part and parcel of the lesson design process. In this case, the teacher selects an existing CAL, package that fits into the overall lesson design and that can be used effectively with existing hardware.

There is, of course, yet another possibility; the teacher may decide to develop the courseware that he needs for his lesson. However, we shall not discuss this level of detail here. Another whole book would be needed.

To deal with the 'macro'decision levels first, we shall consider the course for which CAL, is bring considered, as a SYSTEM. We can then organize our decision making process in terms of;

- *System outputs*-what we hope to gain from the use of CAL that we cannot gain by presently available course methods materials or other viable cheaper innovation;
- *Process factors*- how the use of CAL will change the course in terms of the degree of individualization which will be possible/ desirable, the interaction between student and course materials, the form and degree of control and automated management of the course that will be possible, other effects on student motivation, learning skills, satisfaction, etc.
- *Input factors*-what resources will be required in order to implement CAL as desired-what computer hardware and communication

systems will be necessary, what courseware must be obtained or developed and what human resources will be required in order to get the whole ideas implemented;

- *Contextual factors*-what economic and organizational factors should be taken into account in order to judge the p[notable chances of success or failure of the proposed innovation.

The specific questions that should be considered under each of these four headings are presented in the four reference maps that follow. These maps are designed to be used as job-aids to assist the decision-making process when faced with the possible selection of CAL as a principal medium of instruction for a given course.

5 Computers and the Organisation of Learning

Introduction

During the last five years, as microcomputers have entered schools and classrooms, the educational community has grappled with what computers are and how they should support learning. The classroom use of microcomputers began with computer-assisted instruction, a use very much like workbook-based practice and still quite wide-spread. Computer literacy and programming, which make the technology itself the object of study, have been added to the curriculum in many elementary and secondary schools. Because they are generally taught as separate subjects, sometimes by special teachers in computer laboratories, these literacy programs do not often challenge the organization of learning in regular classroom or in the overall curriculum.

More recently, however, schools have become interested in using tools software-applications programs, such as word processing, which can support classroom work, and which have the potential of changing the nature of that work. In addition, some schools are experimenting with simulations, which support students' exploration of high-level concepts in particular domains, for example, Newtonian physics, economics, navigation. These programs too, have the potential of changing learning in classrooms because of the level of cognitive engagement they support and because of the small-group learning they make possible.

Over the last five years, we have been attempting to understand what the incorporation of microcomputers means for the organization of learning in classrooms. When we began our research, we assumed that we could assess straightforwardly the impact of the technology on classrooms. Now, however, it is clear that the situation we set out to document and understand is not a stable one. The educational functions for the technology and the ways in which they are interpreted by teachers and students are under development. While the technology has the potential of gradually shaping the organization of classroom learning in profoundly new ways, only small changes are visible now. Therefore, current research cannot be conclusive. It can provide important insights into and raise questions about this evolving phenomenon.

At the same times, as teachers and students are trying to make sense of computers, the technology itself is under development. What will be available for schools in fives years is likely to differ qualitatively from what is now on the market. Moreover, the potential cognitive impact of the technology on education has just begun to be envisioned. Well-designed software for educational goals and the cognitive demands that an information age places on us all may change what is taught and learned in fundamental ways.

Practitioners, policymakers, hardware and software developers, and researchers are all at the beginning of a story about computer-based technology and classroom learning. It is a story that should be followed closely since the consequences of current choices can clarify future possibilities. In addition, it is a story whose later chapters should be anticipated now since current decisions will importantly affect how the plot unfolds.

The purposes of this chapter are to describe what we have found out about computers and classroom learning and to discuss some of the longer-term possibilities that may follow from either what we have seen or from projected developments in the technology. We have observed four aspects of the organization of learning that appear to be affected by the incorporation of computers in classrooms the curriculum, learning interactions, classroom management, and the assessment and monitoring of students progress. It is to these elements of classroom life that we will address our discussion of current research and our thoughts about the future.

The organization of learning in classrooms

Our culture pays a great deal of attention to the design and maintenance of formal learning settings-schools and classrooms. The characteristics of these settings represent particular choices about how learning can best be socially organized, within particular constraints. There are shared expectations for how teachers interest with students and how students interact with each other in classrooms.

The overall characteristics of these learning settings have developed over the past two centuries and result from a complex interplay among social. economic, and philosophical factors. Aspects of these settings resist change. These robust features includes, settings where many students are engaged with one adult, open space, curricula divided into subject areas, curriculum organized over time both daily and yearly; and both formal and informal methods for assessing progress. Teachers, parents, and students have well-developed expectations for these learning environments.

Nonetheless, certain features of the formal learning setting are subject to variation among teachers, schools, and districts. Often arising from differing philosophies of learning, these variations encompass arrangements of classrooms, the learning material and subject matter presented, and the method of introducing material and of supporting student's activities. Thus, when looked at closely, each classroom is a novel setting, an interpretation of the formal properties and goals of the educational system uniquely instantiated in practice. As educators experiment with and revise their particular settings, the organization of classroom is, like technology itself, under development.

Therefore, the impact of microcomputer technology on classrooms entails malleability of two kinds; of the technology as it is shaped to educational goals and of classrooms as teachers and students use and interpret the technology in different ways. Neither cognitive nor social impacts can be considered independently of the functions the technology serves and of its meaning for those who use it. That the technology can have a particular impact on classrooms does not necessarily mean that it will. Effective research must examine how the use and meaning of technology are shaped in classrooms over long period time.

Three programs of research

Three programs of research conducted over the past five years shed light on the processes involved in incorporating microcomputers into classrooms. One focused on the incorporation of Logo programming into an elementary and middle-school classroom, the second on the use of prototype mathematics and science software in upper elementary classrooms, and the third on the implementation of database management software in sixth-and eighth-grade classroom. In these projects, important changes were revealed as teachers and students continued working with particular software-changes related to classroom curriculum, learning interactions, classroom management, and assessment and monitoring of student progress.

Earning to program in logo: Over a two-year

period, we conducted a series of studies to understand better the cognitive aspects of learning to program and the social and organizational aspects of incorporating microcomputers and logo into classrooms. Two mixed-grade classrooms is an independent school participated in the research effort-on third-and fourth-grade class and one sixth-and seventh-grade class. Each classroom was equipped with six microcomputers, and logo programming work was incorporated into the ongoing classroom schedule. The organization of the Logo-based learning experience was in the hands of the teachers throughout the two-year experiment.

At the outset of the research in 1981, teachers and schools were just beginning to be enthusiastically engaged with the idea of teaching general problem-solving skills to elementary school students through work with Logo. In-depth research in these classroom over a protracted period allowed us to study in detail the development of students' understanding of programming and the various factors influencing the incorporation of computers into the classrooms.

The use of database management systems for critical inquiry: In another program of research, we have been investigating the potential of computer technology for supporting the development of critical inquiry skills-those skills by which people pose and refine questions and problems,gather and analyze information, and interpret and synthesize material into an informed perspective. We have conducted a series of studies to determine the effectiveness of commercially available information-managing software tools for use in classroom in order to help students learn and practice these skills. We have also examined how these skills are taught in classrooms.

Study of Science and mathematics software: the Project in Science and mathematics Education at Bank Street has, over the past three years, produced a television series and three microcomputer software packages to present science and mathematics concepts to students in fourth through sixth grade. Formative research has played an important role in the development of these materials. Studies have been conducted with individual students and in classroom in order to determine whether the materials appealed to teachers and students and what students learned. research findings have informed the design and revision of the materials.

Research findings and their long-term implications for classrooms

Taken together, our findings suggest that technological innovations take place gradually and are interpreted and shaped by the knowledge, experience, and setting of those teachers and students who encounter them. Thus, such innovations do not necessarily change the educational landscape in standard ways, but offer opportunities to reshape individual settings. From the perspective of how learning is organized, four domains of change seem particularly important to consider: the curriculum, learning interactions, the management of classrooms, and the monitoring and assessment of student progress.

The curriculum

The incorporation of computers into classrooms can present important challenges to the curriculum, challenges that are difficult to resolve. As discussed by Shavelson and his colleagues in a study of how "successful" teachers used microcomputers in relation to mathematics and science curricula, different levels and patters of integration characterized different classrooms. The researchers found that the most comprehensive approach teachers adopted was to use several types of software as an integral part of the curriculum. This "orchestration" of curriculum and software is not simple to achieve. in each of our three programs of research, the implementation of the technology raised issues for teachers and students about its integration into the standard curricular structure.

Logo research: The programming language, logo, did not find a comfortable conceptual home in the curricula of the classrooms. Over the two years of the research it had different relations to the curriculum. At first, it was a specialized learning environment for the development of general problem-solving skills. Then it became a topic in itself-that is, programming. Throughout the two years, teachers experimented with relating Logo to other aspects of the curriculum, such as music, social studies, and science. Initially, the teachers adopted the pedagogy of discovery-based learning associated with Logo-there was no sequence of concepts nor specific expectations for products. Students were encouraged to explore the software and to create their own produces as they chose. Teachers were available to provide help and instruction as needed.

Because logo was a new feature of the curriculum, teachers faced the challenge of how to help students learn with Logo. Over the two years, they tried a variety of means for supporting children's learning, including instructing them in programming concepts, demonstrating how particular techniques could be used in the context of interesting programs, offering completed programs for revision, helping them to develop project ideas, providing completed procedures for use in larger programs, and providing times when students could demonstrate and explain their programs to other students. The computers and Logo were accorded a status different from that of other subjects because the activity lacked a learning sequence and formal expectations for student performance. Teachers and students alike expressed discomfort with this ambiguous status.

At the end of the first year, teachers were dissatisfied with the computer work. They were convinced that the hoped-for learning of learning of general problem-solving skills had not occurred. Teachers observations were supported by research results. When performances of students in Logo classrooms were compared with those of students who had on Logo experience, the result demonstrated no effect of Logo experience on the problem-solving skill of planning. Teachers then shifted their focus to fundamental concepts of computer programming as a curriculum topic. They developed a sequence of instruction which occurred in parallel with students' work on their own programming projects. In this way, links could be made between the teachers' formal instruction and the students' more self-directed activity. For example, students were taught techniques of recursion through several whole-group lessons and could then draw on these concepts for their own projects.

At the end of the second year, teachers were again dissatisfied with what most students had accomplished. Our assessments demonstrated that many children had made relatively little conceptual progress. Teachers were left puzzled about the value of programming for all students and its status in the classroom. Nonetheless, the teachers are today committed to exploring and shaping the potential of computers for classroom use. The recognized that computers were valuable learning tools, but also that they needed to devote significant time to incorporating them into the classroom work. One teacher is continuing to experiment with Logo. During the current school year, he is finding some success in incorporating it into the geometry curriculum as a means of helping children understand basic geometric concepts. He has also been experimenting with other functions for the technology, such as word processing, data management, and simulations. But teachers have developed courses in Logo for adults and other educational uses of computers.

At the close of the experiment, teachers were not fully satisfied with the outcome of the Logo experience for students but concluded that it was valuable to continue to explore it. In addition, the experience convinced them of the utility of the technology for their curricula, motivated them to explore and develop its educational potential further, and made them aware of the complex issues it presented to them as teachers-issues they are still actively confronting.

Database management system research: Intervention studies were conducted in two classrooms to determine whether teachers and students, with support from researchers, could make effective use of database management software as part of their curriculum. This work took place over two months. In a sixth-grade public school classroom, social studies were featured for the database management work. In an eighth-grade public school classroom, science was the featured activity. At the outset of the study, teachers were excited about the potential of this software for helping students to keep their own records and to develop their own research projects. On teacher viewed it as an interesting storage device that would supplement the already well-liked word processor. The second teacher believed that it would help students to develop their own sophisticated queries for a body of information and to record and examine information as a class. Despite their enthusiasm, teachers had difficulty incorporating these tools into the ongoing curriculum work.

Some problems encountered in the course of the research were due to the design of the software, which was intended for business rather than for educational environments. For example, the software designers assumed that students already knew how to organize information hierarchically to set up the database and it did not help them learn how to do so. In addition, many students lost data when they were setting up or exploring files because the software menus were often confusing and the systems did not "protect" students from accidental loss of information.

Apart from these design issues, in the sixth-grade class the software did not integrate well with the social studies curriculum. As opposed to helping students record information from their topic-oriented research projects, the software was designed to store the same pieces of information about multiple cases (for example, population, crops, area, and government of twenty different countries). The teacher had difficulty thinking of ways consistent with her curriculum to make use of this capacity for organizing comparative information. The most obvious uses were not for curriculum but for keeping track of student records and helping students keep journals of their own work. in this class, the principal use of the system became record-keeping; students, kept journals of their weekly work and made notes about progress for each assignment. It was clear that the software would have to be designed differently to support the curriculum goals initially set out.

In the eighth-grade science class, the teacher thought the software could help students to record and compile the results of experiments and to query this information once it had been recorded. While the students and teacher enthusiastically set up data-recording formate and entered their data from an ongoing experiment, this form of working did not readily assimilate into the way the science curriculum was organized. While able to design one experiment that could make use of the software, the teacher found if difficult to conceive of how his typical activities and experiments could make use of the data-recording capacities of the computer. Activities were typically organized as demonstration of a phenomenon or a biological structure rather than as experiments in which data were collected and analyzed. In contrast to what was anticipated, he found that it was the unusual classroom science activity rather than the typical one that could truly make use of the database management capacities of the computer. Only a new approach to science in the classroom would make this software a useful, sensible tool.

Curricular issues were prominent in these two programs of research because we chose to study uses of the technology that had the promise of supporting skills of problem solving and critical inquiry. As such the software did not have an obvious fit with the traditional curriculum. The curriculum in these classroom had to be stretched or modified in some way to accommodate the technological functions. In these cases, adoption of the technology by the classrooms was not a process of simply incorporating new into old, but of reshaping what was there. We were interested in how such stretching of the standard curricular vision, in the direction of higher-order problem-solving skills that will likely be prominent in an information age, would be accommodated by today's classrooms.

Future implications: Education is currently facing the complex problem of adapting to an information age and determining what such and age requires of and makes possible for its young citizens. Central educational questions are raised by the pervasivencess and potential of the new technology. What is important to know? What are the best methods for ensuring deep and flexible learning for all children?

With respect to the curriculum, its content will very likely change when the advantages and implications of the technology for education are carefully addressed. The National Council of Teachers of Mathematics is already calling for such changes in the mathematics curriculum. Educators have been debating about whether and how the technology itself should become a central topic of study for students. These issues will likely develop as the technology itself changes.

More generally, a greater emphasis on thinking and learning skills may occur. If access to vast amounts of information is made possible through the technology, then learning of facts may become less important than understanding structures of information so that appropriate material can be readily found. Skills in finding, synthesizing and interpreting information are likely to become centrally important in the educational process.

While these are goals for teaching now, they are neither strongly emphasized nor well implemented in most classroom. The tasks of designing systems effectively for these uses and of reshaping curriculum appropriately are profound. Our studies suggest some of the difficulties and possibilities posed at the classroom level by new software that does not have an obvious "fit" with current curriculum.

Learning interactions

The technology may support different kinds of learning interactions in classrooms. Two kinds of changes have been noted in some classrooms-the ways in which teachers interact with students in learning situations and increasing emphasis on student's collaborative learning.

Logo research: In our programming studies we investigated both the occurrence and nature of collaborative exchanges among students as they worked. In one study, we did time-sampled observations of students' interactive behaviours as they worked at the computer and compared them with other classroom tasks where they were encouraged to work together. Data were collected at several points in each of the school years. Analyses revealed that students tended to collaborate more-to talk together about their work-when they were working on microcomputer programming tasks than on other classroom tasks. This comparative difference was consistent over time and classrooms.

Other interesting differences in peer-learning arrangements were apparent as the school year progressed. Some students acquired particular expertise with the language, developed an interest in long-term individual projects, and pursued these projects in a focused way for relatively long periods. In addition, they "consulted" with other students to provide expert help on programming problems. Thus, student information exchange included working together, asking for or giving help with a particular problem, and borrowing sections of program-code that another student had developed. This shared code, seldom analyzed by the borrower, was inserted "whole0hog" into his or her project.

Thus, in these classrooms the implementation of Logo appeared to facilitate collaborative exchange among students workingon problems together and, over time, a recognition on the part of students of distributed experitse among their peers-expertise that could be called upon to help with a problem or contribute a "programming product" to an ongoing project. The occurrence of these learning interactions was not unrelated to the ambiguous status of programming relative to other classroom subjects. Teachers and students were unclear about what material individuals should be responsible for knowing, so the exchange of information was not bounded by established expectations about about individual responsibility for knowledge and products.

With respect to teacher interactions with students, teachers indicated that they sometimes had difficulty knowing how to support students' learning with Logo. Particularly during the first year, the teachers were reluctant to intervene in students' work in other than local ways. That is, teacher helped students with particular problems but felt uneasy about providing general lessons or structuring the learning experience for all students in the same way. They were committed to the idea that students needed freely to explore this environment in order to learn. When they noticed students running into problems, they felt that they did not yet have sufficient intuitions about how or whether to go beyond the specific needs of the individual student.

Science and mathematics software research: Once materials were completed in prototype form, each software module was field-tested in classrooms for a month to determine what revisions would make it more usable in the classroom setting. Thirteen classroom in seven public schools took part in the study. All teachers were trained in the use of a particular software module and used the software, television, and print materials as they chose in their classrooms. We observed classrooms as the software was used, interviewed teachers and students, and assessed students' comprehension of concepts and evaluation of the materials. Two software modules were noteworthy for the learning interactions we observed.

One piece of software was a simulation designed to help children learn and use navigational concepts and the geometries involved. The game was designed to be used in a classroom with only one ortwo computers. To play, teams of children must locate themselves on the sea and move to rescue a whale accidentally trapped in the net of a fishing trawler. The collect and interpret information from computer-based navigational instruments to reach their goal.

Because the computer supported the team-based student collaboration, new forms of interaction occurred in some classrooms. The computer structured the experience so that teachers did not have to be centrally involved and could observe children's work or be freed to work individually with other students. While some teams of students worked effectively together, others had difficulty knowing how to distribute the work among themselves. In some teams, one child dominated the work and made the decisions, leaving others confused as to what was happening. The incorporation of all children into effective collaborative work, then, in a design challenge for software developers and an issue for teachers in organizing learning activities.

There were important differences among teachers in how they interacted with students who were using this software. Interactions sometimes changed as teachers and students became more familiar with the software. Of the five different roles observed, two were similar to traditional classroom interactions. The first, demonstrating the software to students and explaining its use, involved typical whole-class instruction. In the second-managing the physical and social demands of the activity - the teacher's interaction with students was similar to that observed when independent work is conducted in classrooms. Between these extremes, however, were three roles that gave the students opportunities for learning interactions with each other and provided the teacher with significant instructional functions. These three roles varied from the teacher's active participation in the game, to her active monitoring of the game, to her being available as resource person when called upon.

Another piece of software-a series of games to teach programming concepts-also produced interesting learning interactions. In, these games, the students learned and practiced the fundamental commands for turtle graphics-learning how to move an object around the screen through single commands and then through strings of commands. The software was relatively straightforward for students to learn and use. In the field-test classrooms, we found that some teachers adopted the strategy of teaching the games to a pair of students. After using the software for a brief period, that pair then taught the game to two new students, and so on, in a "learning chain". This strategy again freed the teacher for other work and provided the instructional advantage of allowing students to encounter the material as teachers of other students.

Future implications. When examined in the long term the nature of learning interactions in classrooms may change dramatically. The technology may support much more collaborative work on the part of students. Because of the increasing opportunities for paired and small group activities, changes in curriculum, and the capacity of the technology to support students' learning of academic content, teachers may need to become less the provides of content-specific knowledge and more the facilitators of students' acquisition of knowledge. Instruction might shift away from emphasis on information-giving to emphasis on helping students to find relevant information, learn how to solve problems, ask questions, think critically, and communicate ideas. This would mean a significant refocusing of the teacher's work. The teachers we worked with valued the opportunities for new learning interactions but found that their implementation posed important questions about how students can effectively learn from each other and how teachers can participate in and support collaborative learning.

The management of classrooms

As some of our research indicates, particular uses of the technology can free the teacher from continual management of large groups of students to concentrate on work with small groups or individuals. The considerable literature on classroom grouping and learning suggests that more effective engagement and learning may occur when students are organized into smaller activity groups, as compared with whole class activities or isolated seat work. Technology can effectively engage individuals or pairs of students while other students and the teacher act as occasional resources. These potential classroom management changes also present problems to some teachers since they offer new ways of conceptualizing the structure of activities in classrooms.

Logo research: The Logo teachers faced two challenges with respect to classroom management: developing a sensible and equitable system of student access to machines and organizing the activities through which students learned how to program. Although the computers allowed teachers to work more flexibly with small groups, they also made it necessary for teachers to organize students' work with the machines. Early in the year, teachers found it effective to assign pairs of students to computers. As students increased their knowledge of each other and of programming, this assignment process broke down and other methods were developed. Teachers also struggled with whether to *require* students to use their assigned time since the status of programming was ambiguous with respect to the curriculum.

In organizing activities through which children learned how to program, teachers had to manage both students' interactions and their own roles in the instructional process. Teachers encouraged students to make use of each other as learning resources, yet they wanted children to solve their own problems rather than ask someone else to do it or borrow another student's code.

Teachers attempted to disallow direct borrowing by requiring that students make changes in borrowed code as they adapted it for their individual projects. This policy proved effective for some students.

How teachers organized Logo learning activities changed considerably over time. At the outset, learning took place in one context: children worked on their own projects at the computers, and teachers provided help as needed. Gradually, other learning organizations were tried and were added to the schedule or abandoned. For example, both teachers added group instructional sessions during the second year because they felt sequenced instruction in programming concepts would be beneficial. One teacher decided that sequenced instruction was more effectively done in the whole group, while the other organized the sessions in small groups according to level of expertise. In addition, both teachers experimented with what they called "group sharing." In these sessions, children presented their programming projects to the whole group and discussed how the projects had been done. One teacher found group sharing to be very valuable and continued the practice; the other dropped it because of lack of student interest.

Database management system research: The information-management software presented a management challenge to the eighth-grade class that was using it for an experiment to which the whole class contributed. While the students were accustomed to performing experiments in small groups, they were not accustomed to assembling the findings of the class as a whole and examining them. The software made possible group information analysis, but neither the teacher nor the students understood how to take advantage of it. When asked to enter their experimental data into the system, many students, accustomed to seeking right answers, used the opportunity to "clean" their data so that it conformed to what other students had reported. The teacher also saw the database as a means for quickly checking the correctness of students' work. While he wanted to assemble the findings of all students and examine them with the class as a whole, he was not sure how to take advantage of the technology to make this feasible in the classroom setting. For example, effective group analysis of data would have required that the group decide on a data-recording format, that individual students or small groups performed experiments and enter their separate data records, and that the group reconvene to examine and interpret the results.

Future implications: With respect to the long term, we envision two likely changes in the management of classroom work. First, computer-based activities such as simulations and many tool uses will make possible and support joint problem-solving activities by students. Teachers may be managing pairs or groups of students rather than conducting the more typical whole-class or individual activity. To manage and support such work effectively requires observational skills different from those teachers normally apply and new intuitions about when and how to intervene in student-based activities, as well as raising questions about how to monitor the progress of individual students.

The second point about classroom management is that the concept of a classroom may change significantly. If computers become effective and efficient systems of learning support, then it may be possible for students to move through material at their own developmental pace. To the extent that this happens, age-graded classrooms may be called into question. Students may be working on their own much more than they do now and be grouped with others in differing ability combinations for particular activities. Moreover, with extensive use of computer-based networks, an important part of "classroom" work could consist of students talking to each other or experts in particular areas across many miles. In other words, the social and temporal structure on how education happens could alter what a teacher must manage, and how.

The monitoring and assessment of student learning

The increasing use of computers raises new issues about the content of and methods for student assessments. If curriculum is altered, if student learning is more individually tailored, and if there are more opportunities for peer collaboration, then keeping track of and understanding what students do and learn become significant challenges.

Since our research was conducted in classrooms where the software was taken on as an experiment, neither expectations for students' learning nor means of assessment had been established. Nonetheless, difficulties with respect to assessment gradually surfaced as we thought about developing research measures for students' learning and as teachers thought seriously about incorporating the software into their classroom curricula.

Logo research: Assessment of student progress assumed importance for teachers when at the end of the first year they became dissatisfied with the accomplishments reflected in students' individual projects. For these teachers, assessment was important for two reasons. First, it structured the experience for students by providing motivation foe involvement and explicit learning goals. Second assessment helped teachers to diagnose students' understanding in order to intervene more effectively. Assessment of programming knowledge of individual students never became a feature of the classroom experience, however. Teachers had a philosophical commitment to the way Logo learning should be practiced and so did not want to subject it to typical tests. In addition, teachers appreciated the collaborative, project-oriented shape that the programming had taken in their classrooms. They were reluctant to interfere by making it an individually accountable subject.

Teachers believed, however, that the assessment issue was one they would have to address if they continued with programming. During the second year, they worked on developing and presenting programming concepts in an organized, sequenced fashion. As part of this conceptual effort, they realized that they did not really know what should be expected of students in terms of programming knowledge, nor when and how to assess it. Teachers recognized that in the absence of better general understanding of the development of programming knowledge it was premature to consider assessment. Yet they were uncomfortable that they had only their own experience and intuitions to guide their information diagnosis of student understanding. At the end of the experiment, teachers were still considering these issues.

Secience and mathematics software research: The field test of the science and mathematics software also raised issues concerning assessment. Since teachers considered this to be an experiment, they did not take on the problem of assessment. Yet some teachers. Since teachers considered this to be an experiment, they did expressed concerns about how such computer-based experiences could be incorporated into a learning situation in which individual assessments help to organize the work. For example, with respect to the navigation simulation, how would teachers know about individual progress when students were working, inextricably, in groups to solve the problems? What were students learning, and how could the situation be avoided in which less skilled students simply relied on the expertise of those more skilled and/or dominant? Second, what kind of non-computer-based measures of student knowledge are appropriate when the learning has taken place in interaction with the technology? What does it mean to transfer knowledge that has been developed in a dynamic medium to the standard modes of paper-and-pencil assessment?

Future implications: In the long term, how teachers measures and keep track of student performance is likely to change in several ways. First, what is measured may change radically. To the extent that the curriculum changes, indicators of successful performance will also be altered. While a move from one specific content to another need not alter measurement, a move toward emphasis on more general thinking and problem-solving skills or toward more abstract skills within a domain must change both standardized and less formal measurement techniques. Teachers will need to devise new ways of knowing how well their students are doing. Determining whether a student is a good problem solver is different from counting how many problems he or she answers correctly. Yet computer-based activity of the more open-ended varieties can itself provide teachers with new insights into what their students can do. There are many anecdotal accounts of teachers who learned new things about their students' capabilities as a result of observing them at the computer.

The second way in which measurement may change is related to the relative role of the teacher and of the machine in this activity. In some versions of the school of the future, the computer manages instruction. That is, the computer assesses student performance in particular areas, delivers the relevant drill or tutorial, and assesses again. Teachers can get detailed report via computer as to how students are doing. They can then decide what else students need. This computer-managed instruction model generally assumes simple drill-and-practice uses of the computer, uses which differ little from what normally happens in classrooms. To the extent that these are effective and free teachers to do more challenging work with students and that the measures themselves are readily interpretable, they may provide useful ways of keeping track of some aspects of students performance.

Much more radical, however, is the potential of "intelligent" computer systems for understanding and diagnosing student performance. Those most optimistic about the potential of such systems believe it will be possible to build instructional systems that include models of the student's understanding of the domain. Based on the student's performance, these models change, and the program behaves appropriately. It may, for example, prompt the student to reconsider an answer, demonstrate a different process foe solving a problem, or ask the student to indicate why she though her response was correct. These programs are intended to work in very much the same way that a sensitive teacher would work in a one-to-one session with the student.

Other types of intelligent systems might help

teachers to understand better students' functioning in particular arenas. For example, one program developed at Xerox PARC analyzes students' errors in arithmetic to reveal a systematic basis of misunderstandings. Such, diagnostic functions, if developed with the needs of teachers in mind, could help teachers zero in much more precisely and effectively on students' conceptual difficulties.

The third way assessment may change relates to increase in joint problem-solving activity in classrooms. If the collaborative, small-group learning that the technology can support is taken seriously, these efforts will have to be assessed. To do so in ways that go beyond simply testing what an individual has learned from a collaborative effort requires new ways of thinking about assessment. Perhaps such thinking can be informed by the world of adult work, where many effort are collaborative and where the results of these efforts are regularly assessed.

We believe that development efforts in this area should proceed from a model that envisions students, teachers, and computers as a collaborative system, as opposed to a model which implies that the computer and the single student constitute a system sufficient for the organization of learning. If teachers are to be effective members of such systems in the future, however, they will have to deal effectively with detailed information about students' difficulties, with the consequences of systems that support more individually tailored student learning, and with both collaborative and individual products.

6 Computers and the Curriculum

Even sober, serious scholars, such as Nobel Laureate Herbert Simon, acknowledge that computers are transforming our world: "Nobody really needs convincing these days that the computer is an innovation of more than ordinary magnitude, a one-in-several-centuries innovation and not a one-in-a century innovation or one of these instant revolutions that are announced every day in the papers or on television." And equally serious academics reach equally extravagant conclusions about the role of computers in education. Consider, for example, this statement by physicist and computer education pioneer, Alfred Bord: "It appears likely that computers will soon be more important in our educational process than books, and, indeed, may entirely replace the book medium for many purposes.

Such revolutionary possibilities inevitably spur a reconsideration of the curriculum of elementary and secondary schooling. What do students need to know about computers and how can this be incorporated into the curriculum? What new content is needed in standard course ir various subjects, like mathematics and science, if students are to be prepared to understand the new technology and to participate fully in the postrevolutionary order of things? What older content may be obsolete?

A considerable body of writing offering answers to these questions has already appeared and more comes off the presses daily. Curriculum materials and textbooks have been developed, tried, revised, and published for teaching computer literacy and computer programming at elementary and secondary levels. The professional societies in mathematics education and science education have already gone on record with their recommendations for changes in their subjects to accommodate the computer revolution. Professional journals contain articles by th dozens. describing innovative curriculum work by teachers, schools, and school systems. Some states have developed master plans for using computers in their schools. There is controversy galore in this literature, and some of the lines of dispute will be touched upon later in this chapter, but there is no shortage of ideas and proposals. One might say that the apparatus of curriculum change is working just as we would hope to prepare for the necessary curriculum changes being ushered in by the computer.

But there is a problem. Little of what is written about in the journals is coming to pass in schools. Even small-scale, partial realizations of the least controversial changes stretch the schools involved to the limits of their capacity for institutional adaptation and change. And these successes, achieved at such cost, will not begin to satisfy the people who advocate the use of computers for education. Thus the stage is set for another in the unbroken series of failures and partial, temporary successes that mark the history of American school reform efforts since the 1950s.

The goal of this chapter is to explain how efforts to use computers for education may affect the curriculum. In this case as in most cases of technologically stimulated change, the indirect effects are likely to be greater than the direct ones, and the ultimate impact is likely to be quite different from what we foresaw. I do not claim any special powers of foresight, but my analysis of the general problem suggests strongly that the crucial issues will be those of implementation, that the impact of computers on schools will depend more on the difficulties of institutional change than on any other set of factors. This analysis begins with the motives that spur so many to advocate the use of computers for education, proceeds to consider some of the many ways schools might use computers, each of which has different implications for curricular impact, then looks at the implementation problems schools will need to overcome in order to use computers, and finally ventures some predictions grounded in these analyses about the possible futures for computers in schools.

The promise of computers for education

No other educational innovation since the

Progressive Education Movement has been received with such intensity and embranced by so wide a spectrum of the educational community and the public. The support received by previous technological innovations-radio, film, television, teaching machines-pales by comparison.

The appeal of the computer can be traced in part to its inherent pedagogical strength. Elsewhere I have identified some of these: more active learning; more varied sensory and conceptual modes; individually tailored learning; learning nearer the speed of thought; and an aid to abstraction. In addition, as a technology, the computer has one very considerable advantage over earlier forms of educational technology-versatility. It can be used in nearly unlimited ways to achieve virtually any educational aim and to conform to virtually any educational philosophy. The same device may be used for drill and practice and for open-ended exploration, used in graduate school and preschool. This versatility earns computers some support from within nearly all communities of belief, opinion, and action.

Computers are controllable by their users to a degree never before seen in any electronic device and to a degree matched only by paper and pencil, chalkboard, and overhead projector among pre-electronic educational aids. And, unlike any previous invention, the computer extends humanity's power of representing and logically manipulating formal systems of all kinds. It is almost as if a new discipline had been discovered, a kind of hyper-mathematics, that encompasses all order and that is capable, therefore, of helping us to recognize and deal with order on a scale of complexity heretofore impossible. Translated into mundane activities, this power of the computer brings us word processors, spreadsheets, database management systems, and a whole panoply of tools for thinking. No other educational innovation has offered anything comparable in power, unless we consider writing, the number system, or speech itself to be educational innovations.

But no cold, clear-eyed assessment of the objective advantages of computers can prepare us for the shining visions we encounter among computer enthusiasts, visions of an unprecedented relation in education. Those who have succumbed to the appeal of such visions will readily appreciate their seductive power. For those who are mystified by it, a bit of explanation may be in order.

One such vision casts the computer as a kind of mental prosthesis or mind tool, magnifying its user's mental capabilities the way microscopes and telescopes extend vision and mechanical machinery multiplies strength. With their aid anyone can do what only a genius could formerly do. For some months in 1983, Allied Corporation ran an advertisement, which showed a 3 x 3 grid of images of eight of the greatest minds of all time-Dante. Shakesoeare. Einstein, Plato....and an electronic chip with the caption: "Of all the world's great thinkers, which is the greatest?" This promise of a technology of intellect catapulting all humanity to new heights of genius is certainly one of the visions responsible for much of the excitement surrounding educational use of computers.

In another vision students have instant electronic access to the entire sum of human knowledge. We hear often how easy it is in principle to put the entire Library of Congress at the fingertips of any computer user, though this is a hopelessly outdated image, because the information needed in today's society grows and changes at a rate that far outstrips our ability to produce and catalog books. The dream of universal access of all knowledge is as powerful a dream as that of universal literacy and universal education. the same energy that built libraries and established schools, colleges, and universities will be drawn to its realization.

A third vision, distinctively education, is that of the personal tutor. An appropriately programmed computer could in principle provide every one with, as Patrick Suppes has claimed, "a tutor as good as Philip of Macedon found for his son." With appropriately programmed computers, students could receive instruction tailored to their personal abilities and preferences, presumably realizing more of their potential than under mass instruction.

To students chafing under requirements imposed by authorities, the personal computer comes as a liberator in much the way the automobile did to an earlier generation. With it they have a whole world to explore, one that has nor already been scoured by generations of adults before them. They can aspire to earn money with their computer skills and to build a foundation of knowledge and skill that can enhance their career prospects later. And to those who believe in the inherent power and goodness latent in every human being, the vision of a personal electronic tool carries some of the same shining promise as other liberating visions in the traditions of Rousseau, Thoreau, and Progressive Education.

Finally, computers hold out the promises of a substantial improvement in the productivity of education, increasing the return on our educational investment. We read how agriculture has increased its productivity many times since preindustrial times, while the productivity of education has not increased at all. We note that in all our basic industries technology has served as the foundation for productivity improvements that have lowered the cost of products and services and thereby made them accessible to more people, leading to increased markets and further cost decreases in a positive spiral of economic development. Meanwhile, in labour intensive sector such as education costs rise relative to the lowering costs of these other commodities and output remains the same or declines, a phenomenon economists call "the cost disease." Christopher Evens stated the crucial issue succinctly: "Universal, personal medical care and personal, dedicated tuition are clearly marvelous goals for the world to aim at, but they are economically attainable even in the richest societies." In this last vision, universal computer-based medical diagnosis and universal tutoring by computer will be economically attainable and will thus help to usher in an age of universal plenty.

These visions are not merely idle fantasies, either. For thirty years pioneering computer educators have laboured to create working educational programs that realize their visions. Seymour Papert developed the computer language/environment, Logo, and supervised experimental programs in the Brookline Schools. Alfred Bork has established the Computer Learning Centre at the University of California at Irvine where dozens of tutorials in physics have been developed. patrick Suppes has developed a complete computer-based curriculum though high school. The innovative PLATO experiment in computer-based learning founded at the University of Illinois is now offered commercially by Control Data Corporation. The WICAT Foundation, in provo, Utah, operates a school that uses computers intensively as an integral part of its program. Although their visions are far from being realized, these pioneers and the settlers who have followed them have demonstrated some significant progress.

Computers are also a source of deep fears, nightmares, if you will. Some fear what Lewis Mumford called "the mechanomorphism of man"-that humanity will be thought of as nothing more than a machine. Some individuals feel that they may be inadequate in using computers and some that they may be replaced by computers in their jobs. But at least as common are fears to what may happen if one does not learn to use computers. This fear goes beyond economics: the loss of business or job opportunities or even the displacement of whole industries by competitors abroad. It includes far of domination by those whose power has been augmented through computers. It also includes fear of loss of self-esteem and status: in an age of information those who do not use the new technologies risk being labelled as backward and obsolescent.

Computers come to education astride some powerful dreams, drams as strong as those that powered the creation of school systems in the first place. These visions give the computer an uncanny appeal that activates social energy and attracts attention in amounts matched by no other educational innovation. And it is this social energy that makes the computer so important. Because they generate such visions, computers are indeed the ingredients of revolution.

Way to use computers for education

Because of the tremendous aura of hopes and fears that surrounds computers in the public mind, the question of whether to use computers for education is not, in my mind, a serious issue. Yes, it will be debated. Even quite prominent figures will lament the intrusion of machines into our mental lives, just as Plato lamented the intrusion of reading and writing into the predominantly oral intellectual life of his time. But people will continue to find uses for computers in education just as they continued to find uses for reading and writing. The issue of how computers should best be used for education is, however, not moot.

Much of the present debate about how to use computers for education follows well-worn ideological lines. On the right, representing traditional educational ideas, are such use s as drill and practice on basis skills, tutorials on fundamental concepts, and simulations of basic processes in the natural and social sciences. On the left, representing progressive educational ideals, are such uses as exploring a microworld, learning to solve problems using software tools, and carrying out personal or group projects on the computer.

Differences of opinion about computer-based practices split along many of the same philosophical lines as those about conventional educational practices. The debates about BASIC versus Logo, for example, or drill-and-practice versus tools could, with only light editing, be applied to didactic teaching versus discovery learning or content coverage versus problem-solving skills. Ideological struggles such as these will continue, but I doubt that they will resolve anything because their differences stem from different ideals, visions, if you will.

Educational practices are linked to the visions computers generate. The vision of computers as mind tools can be pursued by using formula-solving programs on otherwise intractable mathematics or science problems. The ideal of a personalized tutor can be pursued by using adaptive programs in computer-assisted instruction. Thatching the masses to program in an easily learned computer language can be viewed as moving to ward the ideal of liberating them from domination by a techno-elite. Using a modem to access a database can be seen as a step in the direction of universal knowledge access. Using a computer to monitor the progress of all the students in the school can be seen as step toward increased educational productivity. While advocates of computers, agree on their value and on the position that they should be used, they disagree-often violently-on how to use them. Their disagreements are not primarily about facts; research results showing that one use produced better results with students than another would still leave the disputants debating which results mattered the most.

Different uses of computers have quite different implications for the curriculum. Widespread use of drill-and-practice software is consistent with the predominant emphasis on learning of facts and skills in our schools. If computers were used for drill and practice part of the time and the rest of school time were spent in classrooms on other objectives, such as higher-order thinking skills, and affective and psychomotor learning, the purposes and content of most elementary and secondary school could be accommodated. But this would mean a complete overhaul of instructional patterns in the classroom. Teachers would assume different roles; the pattern of communication and social interaction would have to change. Textbooks, if they were used at all, would have to be drastically revised. The tendency would be to displace for some time each day the conventional teacher-centered, talk-oriented, whole-class activity pattern of classroom interaction with a materialize-centered, activity-oriented, individualized one, and to orient remaining classroom activities towards other educational objectives, leaving the content and purpose of education otherwise unchanged.

Computers could be used as intellectual tools with theframework of a conventional classroom. For example, the computer could be used as an audio-visual device by the teacher in lectures or whole-class activities or as an aid to individual students in doing their assigned work outside the class, as reference books or calculators are used. Students could work on computers individually or in groups, but would eventually need to discuss their work and findings among themselves and with teachers, and thus this work would be integrated into the rest of the course. If this use of computers were to become widespread, more instructional emphasis would eventually be placed on developing a solution plan, less on execution. Textbooks and tests would need to be revised to reflect increased emphasis on planning solution strategies and decreased emphasis on carrying them out mentally or on paper. Also, many of the oversimplified "textbook" problems currently the staple of most quantitative courses could be replaced by more realistic ones, since it is no easier for the computer to work with round numbers or simple formulas than with more complex data. Courses which currently lack an intellectual focus-industrial arts, home economics, physical education-could be revised to emphasize the use of appropriate computer tools in their activities.

If the use of computers as tools should prove markedly successful in augmenting the intellectual power of students at an early age, it could make today's rigid age grading infeasible. The gap between the best performing and poorest performing students would be widened. On the other hand, it might become more difficult to persuade youngsters to labur after understanding of principles when "the computer can do it." Just as language and mathematics skills strongly influence school performance in all subject, so facility in the use of these tools would, too. Seeing this, schools would want to provide explicit instruction in their use. Such instruction might become a major part of the curriculum in its own right or a central ingredient in other courses and subjects. This use of computers would entail a shift in the priorities of schooling in a more intellectual and cognitive direction, and it could undermine the age-graded structure; but it would probably not otherwise make substantial changes in curriculum.

Readers can easily see for themselves that widespread adoption of computers would require far-reaching adjustments in the purpose, content, and structure of schools. The enormous energy generated by the far-reaching visions of computer-based education expresses itself in an arry of competing uses, each of which demands different changes from schools. How schools use computers and how computers influence learning depend more upon our willingness and ability to make the requisite changes than upon the claims made for this or that use. And so we come to the implementation issue.

The challenges of implementation

As the foregoing discussion suggests, using computers poses some severe challenges for those responsible for curriculum work in schools. New courses must be developed. Room must be found for them in the schedule. New units must be developed and added to an already crowded schedule. Software and print materials must be selected or developed. Teachers must be found who are qualified to teach the new material. Teachers' guides and support materials must be produced. Classroom techniques must be devised that enable all teachers to use computers effectively in ways that help all students reach computer-related goals. None of these is an easy on straightforward task, and failure at any of them is materially and emotionally costly for teachers, parents and students.

Each school and each school system in the country is making or will have to make a series of decisions about using computers: How much use?

What kinds? With what goals? Who will be involved? When and where will this take place? How much will it cost, and how will the cost be paid? Policy decisions on these issues have their own costs and risks. A decision to use computers or not in each of the many possible ways must wend its way through whatever curriculum decision process a school or school system may have. Normally there will be advocates of various computer-based programs both inside and outside schools. There may also be opposition. Resolving these conflicts will require time, energy, and attention and brings risks of lasting political and social divisions. There will certainly be competing claims for the resources needed to offer computer-based programs. The resources required for most computer-based programs are large by comparison with curriculum material budgets generally, and reallocation of existing resources in certain to squeeze current users of these resources. Thus, conflicts over resource become more likely. Maintaining equity of computer access among users is certain to be a continuing additional responsibility of school leaders. Managing the resources places added demands on the curriculum management system. Again, failures in these tasks have real and serious consequences for the individuals and organizations involved.

Beyond schools, publishes of curriculum materials must produce new titles reflecting computer usage. If they move too fast or far, or not fast or far enough, they risk losing markets and profits. Revisions are needed in standardized tests as well as in textbooks, workbooks, and other curriculum materials. The most pressing need, of course, is for software to support these various uses of computers. Various forms of research and evaluation will be demanded by policy makers to check claims made for and against computer-based programs and to discover ways to use them more effectively. New forms of teacher preparation will have to be devised to teach beginning teachers as well as those already in service how to use computers in their work.

These are major undertakings, but arrangements have long been in place for doing them. Curriculum changes of this soft are made routinely by those charged with responsibility for curriculum work within the existing systems. The existence of these standing arrangements for curriculum change is a fact of profound importance for understanding the impact of computers on the curriculum. Decisions about the sue of computers well be made n the same way that decisions about other requiring changes in school programs are now made. When educational uses of computers must find their way into schools through these conventional decision-making channels, a premium is placed on those uses that interfere least with the existing pattern. If radical change can not be avoided, they will be confined to one part of the program so that a new thing can be added or substituted for something else without disturbing the overall pattern. Changes that require widespread adjustments throughout the system will encounter resistance al along the way.

Also, the existing apparatus requires consensus: anything vigorously opposed is thereby defeated. In short, the standard arrangements for curriculum change will tend to shape the use of computers to suit the existing school system.

Thus, adding a course on computer programming or computer literacy is an action schools are set up to take. Colleges are accustomed to deciding if a new course should be required or if it can be counted against their entrance requirements. State departments of education know how to develop guidelines and syllabi for new courses. Certification agencies are familiar with writing standards for the preparation of teachers in a new subject. Publishers know how to develop textbooks for new courses. By contrast, teaching children to use computer graphics as a tool for visual thinking and communication, although its ultimate educational benefit might be greater, faces as much more uphill battle. In which courses would it fit? How would we test for it? Would it be seen as a challenge to the primacy of literacy and numeracy, a threat to the English and mathematics departments? Would colleges treat it like art or like english or neither or both? What kind of book would be suitable for such instruction? The proposal is likely t fail because of incompatibility with the decision-making structure.

I have before me now an advertisement for a computer network which illustrates this vividly. It shows a photograph of high school classroom. Students sit at their individual desks acing the front of the room. The teacher stands at the front of the class before a green chalkboard. On each desk is a computer. The teacher is talking, and the students are watching their computers. On each computer is the same message.

It is, I think, the implementation problems that will determine the type and extent of uses to which computers are put in schools, not the philosophical or theoretical claims and not the objective benefits to be gained from any given use. Put simply, so long as matters proceed through the existing channels of change in school programs, only those uses of computers will be implemented that do not disturb the older, more accepted, tried-and-true ways of doing things.

It is possible that existing arrangements may be circumvented. This might happen in any of three distinct ways: by overloading them, by intervention from higher authorities, and by competition from other educative agencies. The existing arrangements may be overloaded by the size and variety of the problems computer applications pose to the many parts of a school system. These problems and their demands are unusual, perhaps unprecedented. Imagine a school system in which there are not sufficient funds to buy even one computer for every classroom, no budget for software, at best one teacher in ten who knows how to use computers, pressure from parents and some teachers to use computers, and resistance from other parents and teachers ranging from "I have questions about it" to "We must defend the school from the techno-barbarians." Imagine carrying out all the planning and implementation required for computer-based education in such an environment. Yet even the best prepared schools in th country face many of these problems. Taken together and all at once, the problems of implementing any computer-based program on a widespread basis are immense, so immense as to create a danger of overwhelming the institutional arrangements by which schools manage curriculum change.

Most likely, the result of overloading will be to leave decisions to individuals, avoiding an institutional response that can in any even never be adequate. This, I think, is the situation at present in most school systems in the country. In this event what happens is:

1. slow, haphazard, and scatted acquisition of equipment;
2. use by a few enthusiastic teachers who become specialists;
3. use in isolated individual courses;
4. improvisation, year-to-year adjustment;
5. highly variable quality.

In short, if the institutional mechanisms cannot cope with the demands for decision and action about using computers in the schools, the uses will develop on a small-scale, grassroots level in respect to individual initiatives. Use of computers will remain at the periphery of the institution not affecting its core activities, just as other forms of technology-films, video, tape records, and so forth-do today. Should computer use grow to a point where its effects on core school activities were substantial, it would surely demand more regularization and control. If not, significant progress might still be made toward some of the entrancing visions of computers in education, though it would certainly be slow and would affect only a few students in small ways.

The existing arrangements can be overpowered by the intervention of higher authorities or more powerful organizations. The most successful historical example of use of the overpowering strategy is found in the political actions of supporters of vocational education around the turn of this century. Failing in their efforts to persuade school leaders to adopt vocational education on the scale they believed necessary, leaders of the movement organized political support through the National Society for the Promotion of Industrial Education. With support from powerful industrialists and widespread popular support they managed to have laws enacted in key industrial states which mandated vocational education and allocated funds for it. Eventually they secured passage of a federal law allocating funds to schools on the condition that vocational education programs be established; they then wrote the regulations which ensured that new personnel sympathetic to vocational education would be put in charge of the new programs. Supporters of the use of computers might also seek the aid of a greater power outside the normal channels of school decision making.

This could be government once again, or a consortium of states, or networks of business and community organizations.

Perhaps the most promising strategy for computer visionaries is to establish alternative educational agencies that are not so encumbered with tradition. Clearly, it is easier to build a computer-using educational program from scratch than it is to convert an existing school to the use of computers. In building from scratch one can choose qualified personnel without regard to seniority, and one can sidestep many of the regulations concerning pay, promotion, and certification that entangle schools. In addition, the founders are free to shape their program to suit their own educational values provided only that a clientele can be found who will support the program.

Several institutions are responding in imaginative ways to local demands for computer education. The Institute for Computer Technology in Sunnyvale offers a full program of courses in al aspects of computers-design, operation, repair, programming, use of application programs-to any resident of the participating school districts. Its faculty do not have to be certified teachers. It has no "permanent" staff. Its policy is made by a board consisting of representatives of local businesses who also provide partial funding.

A second example of an alternative educational agency is a private for-profit organization, Edupro, in Palo Alto. This organization combines classes for elementary and preschool youngsters after school, weekends, and holidays with educational software development. Still another example is the Lawrence Hall of Science in Berkeley. It offers a rich array of classes for youngsters of all ages some of which are offered during the day for students who are bussed in from their schools. There are other classes for the public on weekends, holidays, and after school. In such programs innovative content is presented and innovative methods are used which would be difficult to sustain in an ordinary school environment. These practices seem to reach nearer to dreams of the computer's potential as an educational medium and support a belief that the visions may indeed be realizable.

If even a small part of the visionary dreams of computer-based education is to be realized, major changes will be required in the day-to-day activity and interaction patterns in classrooms around the country. New computer-using classroom patterns or new forms of schooling in which conventional classrooms do not play the starring role will have to be developed. Developing these new patterns will require collaborative effort on a large scale sustained over a decade or more. Implementing successful patterns will require huge investments in in-service education and a revamping of preservice teacher education programs. Results of this sort will not be achieved solely through the individual efforts of talented teachers or through the gradual accertion of computer-using activities and courses within schools that otherwise continue to operate as they always have. All that piecemeal reform is likely to bring us is computer literacy, programming, and computer-assisted instruction as an occasional adjunct to select classes.

The difficult work of developing innovating computer based programs requires a concentration of collaborating innovators in supportive settings where developing the new pattern is the primary institutional focus. We can expect therefore, the appearance of new organizational entities within which program development will take place. These could be units within schools or independent agencies. Independent organizations could contract with schools to develop and test computer-based programs. Teachers in the school could be employed part time by the new organization. Or such organizations could seek legislative charters as publicly supported agencies that operate with some degree of independence from the existing system. Alternatively, these new settings could consist of networks or coalitions of collaborating local organizations funded by grants as well as by offering their services directly to the public. Such organizations would have much more flexibility in responding to computer-related educational demands, though their existence would be less secure. They may turn out to be merely temporary systems like those created in earlier curriculum reform movements-The Physical Science Study Committee or the Science curriculum Improvement Study, or Britain's National Development Programme for Computer-Assisted Learning. They may be co-opted within the existing system when and if they succeed. Or, they may attain secure independence as new forms of education. The outcome cannot be predicted; however, the developmental part of computer education is less likely to take place within conventional schools and classrooms than in special environments established to nurture innovation.

Whether or not alternative schools thrive, they will serve a vital function as hothouses for development. If they produce programs with noticeably superior results-if, for example, the Writing-To-Read program were to live up to hopes for it-then these programs will spread either to traditional schools or through networks of alternative educational agencies. Stanley Pogrow predicts "environmental collapse"-withdrawal of public support-if schools do not move vigorously to take advantage of the promise of the new technology. But even if nothing so apocalyptic should occur, computers, if effective, will provide students and their parents another educational option, and this in itself will make schools more responsive to their clients.

What will happen?

We can learn something of what many happen from a close look at what is already happening. These past few years have seen the number of schools with computers vault from a negligible number to over 75 percent of all schools by 1983-84. Some patterns of computer use are becoming quite widespread. Fortunately, these developments have been well monitored, and we can already begin to see faint outlines of a national pattern of computer use in schools.

The basic findings are:

1. Teaching about computers is th dominant use of computers in schools today.
2. Drill and practice is the most common form of teaching something else with computers.
3. All other applications of computers, such as their use as tools or as learning aids in academic subjects, are relatively rate.
4. Some new computer-related content is becoming common in other parts of the curriculum, notably set theory, logic, binary arithmetic, and Boolean algebra, in mathematics; social issues and the history of computers in social studies; and electronics in science.

These results reflect the relative ease of adapting various uses to existing school practice. Given pressures to "joint the computer revolution" together with a limited supply of computers, adequate software, and qualified teachers, the easiest response for a school is to put the computers in a computer centre, put the most qualified teacher(s) in charge, and have them offer courses or units on computer literacy, computer programming, and other forms of teaching about computers. For teachers, the easiest response is to take the whole class to computer centre regularly for work on the computer, and the most easily understandable and justifiable work to have them do is drill and practice on basic skills. Anything else requires more money, more effort and expertise from teachers, and more variance from existing school practices.

When we look at the decision-making and change processes that accompany the use of computers in schools, we find several intriguing developments. First, we find teachers with expertise in the use of computers moving into specialized roles as directors of computing, computer consultants, coordinators, and the like. Second, we find that computer-related decision making is often bypassing the school's ordinary decision-making apparatus. Computers are purchased with funds from various sources other than the regular school budget. in some communities parents are organizing foundations, to assist schools with projects that require funds above and beyond those in the regular school budgets; in these communities computers and software are often purchased from these funds. In some communities businesses are assisting schools to develop computer-based offerings. Teachers are initiating programs with the tacit approval of administrators but in advance of the usual coordinated school or district plan. Rather than waiting for districts to offer in-service education, enterprising teachers are developing their own expertise. Many obtain their own computers for use in their classrooms, often with the assistance of parents with children in their classes. And so we find that computer-based programs in each school reflect the personnel and history of that school. In some schools computers are located in the library and supervised by librarians, in other schools they are located in the mathematics department, in other schools in the science department; some elementary schools distribute their few computers widely among all students and teachers, others concentrate them on the gifted, on special education students, or on other groups of students. The practices followed usually reflect the preferences of a principal or a few computer-qualified teachers.

Third, there are signs that the curriculum decision-making arrangements are beginning to be overloaded. Demands for time, energy, money, and especially for knowledge and expertise are already far in excess of the ability of the schools to respond. Most schools are scrambling to provide enough hardware, software and training to mount their computer-based programs. Few teachers of computer programming have credentials in any way comparable to teachers of other school subjects. Teachers who develop expertise are quickly snapped up either for administrative jobs as computer coordinators or for jobs in business and industry. Few school systems have yet been able to found software libraries and run them as systematically as their audio-visual libraries or their libraries of print materials are run. Neither supporters nor opponents have yet organized effective constituencies. In short, the computer revolution has overtaken the schools from so many sides with such violent rapidity that they struggle simply to cope with all the changes that must be considered. The implementation problem is already proving to be the bottleneck.

For the rest of this decade the development of computer use in schools is almost certain to continue in patterns already apparent. Elementary school strands in computer literacy and Logo will become established nationwide, and experimentation with other uses-especially word processing-will continue and expand in selected schools. In secondary schools, courses in computer programming and computer applications of various kinds will become standard offerings, and more computer-related content will seep into existing subjects. Thus a secure niche for computer-based learning will become established in both elementary and secondary schools. These developments will be achieved at great cost and with great difficulty in out schools, yet they will barely touch the academic and vocational core of either the elementary or the secondary schools and will prove deeply disappointing to advocates of computer-based education.

The contrast between the visions of computer education advocates and the realities of how computers are actually being used in schools could hardly be more stark. The visionaries and their followers are certainly not going to be happy with a computer-based education program that consists of computer literacy, turtle graphics, and programming in BASIC. Such changes do not engage the dreams that energize people to work toward computer-based education. They are predictable responses of a bureaucracy-unimaginative to the point of stodginess, bland, and superficial. And yet schools are pressed almost beyond coping just to provide these feeble responses to the computer challenge.

Advocates of computers will surely not give up trying to realize their visions through the schools. They will pursue all their options: reforming schools through existing channels, circumventing those channels from below with grassroots reform movements and from above with power plays to higher authorities or more powerful institutions, an developing competing alternatives. How much effort is devoted to each of these options will likely depend on th success obtained each. My guess is that the establishment of alternative and the cultivation of the grassroots will be most effective initially. When successful programs have been demonstrated under realistic field conditions, both regular schools channels and higher powers will be more receptive.

Conclusions

I see the classroom as an artificial and inefficient learning environment that society has been forced to invent because its informal environments fails in certain essential learning domains, such a writing or grammar or school mathematics. I believe that the computer presence will enable us to so modify the learning environment outside the classrooms that much if not all the knowledge schools presently try to teach with such pain and expense and such limited success will be learned, as the child learns to talk, painlessly, successfully, and without organized instruction. This obviously implies that schools as we know them today will have no place in he future.

I cannot agree with those who foresee death of organized school certainly not in this century. In any future we will need a place for out children: homes are still emptying during the day. And we will want them to spend their time well, but not in economically productive ways that will take adult jobs. We will want them closely supervised. So we will have something like schools. On the other hand, I cannot imagine that we or our children will continue to be satisfied with as much stereotyped talking and listening as go on in school today or as much passive reading and rudimentary writing. Not if it is possible to do better with computers cheeply and easily. I feel certain that computers will be used for education. The energy generated by the visions of new educational possibilities ensures this. And so we will have schools that use computers.

But we must get from here to there. What we have now are decidedly imperfect schools struggling to maintain the quality of the education they offer under deteriorating conditions. Can we transform them into th electronic schools of the future? Not without a lot of work, skill, and luck. Will new educational institutions arise and displace them? They will certainly arise. They may be displace the schools of today, or they may only show them how to be successful in using computers. To reform the schools, either directly or by computations from alternative schools, will leave us with a school system that is a public institution governed politically. Displacement by alternative schools will leave us with a private school system driven by the market. Such indirect institutional changes would have greater imp[act in the curriculum than more direct effects, but it is impossible to predict them. They depend upon the choices we make individually and with our political institutions in the coming decade.

Whatever happens, computers "will have profound effects in our institutions, our teachers, and even our way of life." Perhaps the metaphor of revaluation is as appropriate as the visionaries suggest.

7 Computers and the Educational Programme

Because of rapid changes in recent years, changes influenced by the microchip, the task of preparing this chapter more than a year prior to publication has become a formidable one. The writers were particularly aware of Einstein's wisdom as they confronted the speed of "knowledge creep" in the realm of microelectronics and education. The microchip, in effect, has fertilized education with a host of electronic genes-and done so with mesmerizing speed.

This chapter provides background information deemed to be of importance as society moves into the microelectronic environment of the future. Initially the flow of several major streams in computer development is examined. These range from early historical developments to microelectronic marvels which are still on the drawing boards.

After giving passing attention to the social and educational turbulence that is permeating our lives as a result of the silicon age, the chapter focuses on some of the implications of microtechnologies, particularly the phenomenon of networking and the need for changes in the preparation of professional educators. A concluding section, written with a blend of pragmatism and intuition, treats some of the cautions and caveats educators may need to keep in mind as they seek to catch their breath in the midst of hectic changes.

Contemporary developments in the microelectronic era

A number of years ago, Daniel Bell, the Harvard sociologist, forecast that an emerging "service society" would surface as machines began to replace muscle power on the farm and in the factory. Bell envisioned a service society elbowing its way past the industrial era because there was no way to anticipate the impact of a microelectronic information epoch which was still in its early infancy. By 1980, however, as Japanese scholar Yoneji Masuda pointed out, the postindustrial period had turned into an information rather than a service society. This information society in its turn is changing into a knowledge-based society, with wide ranging implications for education, work, and leisure as well as for life and leadership.

The field of microelectionics emerged rapidly after 1946 when ENIAC, the first digital computer became operable. In the thirty years that followed, the number of works who disseminated knowledge grew rapidly, and by 1977 the information economy employed approximately 50 per cent of the population including computer operators, teachers, media personnel, and the like.

If we assume that ENIAC marked the birth of an information age in 1946, it seems reasonable to contend that the information society reached its lusty youth by 1956-1957. In 1956, as John Naisbitt points out, a "megashift" from the industrial or "smokestack" society took place. In that year, for the first time, blue-collar workers were outnumbered by people in white-collar jobs. Then in 1957, a global communications revolution began when "the Russians launched Sputnik, the missing technological catalyst in a growing information society".

Stages of computer development

We now direct attention to three discernible phases of development in the history of computers and speculate about further developments.

Stage one. The first computers were essentially mechanical contraptions. Development began with the introduction of the abacus in ancient China and flowered in medieval times with the invention of mechanical clocks. The seventeenth-century philosopher-mathematician, Gottfried von Leibnitz, viewed calculation as an activity unworthy of people as intelligent as himself. As a result, he developed a mechanical counting device to save time. His invention, with its stepped wheels, became the mechanical heart of many of the calculating machines used until the early 1970s.

Mechanical calculator technology reached its creative peaks in the mid-nineteenth century. Charles Babbage, a British engineer born in 1791, and ada, Countess of Lovelace, designed a mechanical device capable of processing information in the manner of modern computers. Ada Byron, like her mother a gifted mathematician, is credited with creating the first programming system.

Stage two. After the mid 1940s the second stream of computer development created an increasingly sophisticated and expensive alternative to mechanical calculators, one epitomized by ENIAC. And, so rapid did the accelerating rate of change become after World WAR II, that ENIAC was virtually obsolete by the time it was completed.

In 1947, Bell Laboratories developed the transistor, using in the process tiny pieces of semiconductor material such as silicon and germanium. This development made it possible to combine many circuits in a tiny fraction of the space required by vacuum tubes- and at greatly reduced cost. Another significant even occurred in 1959 when integrated circuits were devised. These involved single chips, each of which contained several complete electronic circuits.

By 1970, when the microchip made its debut, thousands of integrated circuits could be placed on a silicon chip 6.35 mm. square, roughly the size of a child's fingernail. As of the 1980s, over 100,000 transistors can be integrated on a single microchip, each of these bits of silicon containing the same computing power as the original thirty-ton ENIAC. Examples of recent hyperminiaturization ventures include the following: (1) In 1983, Professors Kenneth Hanck and Keith De Armond of North Carolina State University were undertaking to replace microchips with individual molecules capable of storing information in one-millionth of the space silicon chips require; (2) in 1984, Digital Research announced a single computer disc capable of preserving the entire contents of Encyclopedia Britannica; (3) in 1984, work was underway at Cornell University to etch salt crystals with words ten nanometers high which, if successful, would permit putting the contents of Encyclopedia Britannica on a bit of hardware approximately the size of a postage stamp. At the same time, small magnetic bubbles were being incorporated in the microchip to create VLSI eircuitry. These bubbles increase tenfold the present huge memory capacity of the chip. Furthermore, unlike conventional chips, when power-flow is interrupted, information continues to be stored in the chip-memory, ready for retrieval as needed.

Dramatic changes are also taking place in conventional chip technology. Currently chips are made by preparing slices or wafers of silicon four inches in diameter. Up to 400 chips are then chemically etched on to the wafer, the memory and processor of cutting up chips and then putting them together is wasteful of time and money and places limitations on a computer system because of the physical distance electric signals must travel between chips on the board. A way has now been found to use the whole wafer with memory

and processor and thus avoid all the separate steps. This will result in computer systems that are twenty times faster, less power hungry, more compact, and less expensive. In addition, the wafer will have a fail-safe mechanism that will enable it to reconfigure itself automatically so as to eliminate failed chips. Such a development lays the groundwork for the third stage of development.

Stage Three. A promising development in microelectronic technologies, one applicable to the computer field, is just getting underway. Conceivably, the shift will be as dramatic as the shift from mechanical to electronic systems. The new technology uses laser beams in lieu of electric current to permit the creation of optical computers. Their novel characteristic is the use of transphasors, which will function as the equivalents of transistors. In a transistor, a small electric current is used to switch an electric voltage between a high and low value. The high voltage is equivalent to 1 in the binary system and the low to 0. The transphasor performs the same function as the transistor but uses a laser beam which enables it to operate several hundred times faster than the already fantastic nanosecond speed of the transistor- and with greater versatility.

It is becoming apparent as we more closer to the 1990s, that the new "Third Stream" generation of optical computers should have many advantages over earlier models. Optical computers will be much faster, and programming will not longer be confined to binary arithmetic since transphasors can represent more than high and low values. Even more important, the new breed of computers promises to be able to carry out a number of different operations simultaneously. Daniel Bell recently estimated that human knowledge, at its 1983 rate of accumulation, would be doubling every two years by 1992. it seems fortunate, therefore, that future pocket-sized transphasor computers can be (1) inexpensively produced, (2) capable of performing multiple operations simultaneously and (3) freed from the constraints of binary programming, thus promising to help us cope with accelerating change and proliferating information.

Computer futures: the present generation. Sine the development of the first two modern computers in 1946, there has been a phenomenal growth in their number and in their acceptance as efficient and indispensable tools. In 1956, there were about 600 computers. They grew in number to around 30,000 in 1966 and 400,000 in 1976. Today, there are over six million of them, and it is estimated that by 1990 more than half the households in America will invested in computer systems.

As might be expected, opinions vary as to the speed and extent of the proliferation of computers. Peterson and Turkel remind us that as of 1984-85.

Computer makers are cutting prices by the bushel, and... suppliers are laying off workers by the thousands...

The computer revolution will not begin until

small computers reach a stage of development that meets the expectations of... potential business and home users.

They contend that the "dream machine" people seek will need to handle expensive and exasperating jobs and will have greater ease of use. Many people still hesitate to buy equipment because they feel that "today's computers are like model T Fords - revolutionary but slow and awkward".

REgardless of conflicting views as to the precise rate of their penetration, computers are rapidly becoming in integral part of our lives. They are to be found in the factory, farm, and office; the sore, bank, and hospital; the school, university, and home. Society has constructed for itself the "electric surround" foreseen by Marshall McLuhan in the early 1960s. Further progress, however, depends upon the development of a computer systems and already become a barrier to many applications. Most areas of professional activity involve expertise of one kind or another in decision making. The development of computers and associated programs that will effectively simulate professional decision making is only now beginning. A research on "artificial intelligence" begins to make an impact, there should be major forward leaps in fields ranging from education to medicine.

Toward a fifth-generation computer. In the diverse phases of computer development each generation marks a distinct stage in technological advance. As noted earlier, the first generation of computers utilized vacuum tubes; the second, transistors; the third, microchips; and today's fourth generation, extremely powerful superchips. These rapid developments through four generations represent remarkable progress in the refinement of microelectronic technologies.

Current attempts to develop a fifth-generation computer system for the 1990s-one capable of operating intelligently in a manner somewhat like that of the human brain-may demand a radical rethinking of basic educational principles as well as the development of entirely new coping skills on the part of both students and adults as they move into a more complex "electronic surround". Present-day computers do what they are programmed to do, neither more nor less. They have become remarkably efficient tools for learnes, teachers, and school administrator. The development of "intelligent" fifth-generation computer systems offers not only the likelihood of enhanced efficiency, but, even more important, increased effectiveness.

Thee is also the prospect of potential increases in the task of coping with the social turbulence created by the microchip. A potential for hyperturbulence lies in the development of a computer system which is capable of operating intelligently in a manner rather like that of the human brain, capable of "thinking" for itself. if this comes to full fruition, silicon will in effect take over from carbon the current building block of human evolution.

Coping with hyperturbulence generated by the microchip

Before beginning to probe some of the implications of microtechnologies for education, we will consider briefly a few aspects of the hyperturbulence generated by technological developments over the past forty or fifty years. Because of the focus of the present volume, we shall give particular attention to the social hyperturbulence that has occurred since the microchip breakthrough a dozen years ago-a breakthrough which enabled a transportable home computer to be sold at a price within the scope of many family budgets.

The genesis of hyperturbulence. Hyperturbulence in a social environment is a term which describes "the condition that results when available resources and institutions prove inadequate to deal with the speed and diversity of change"

While rapid, unsettling changes are not a unique concomitant of an information society, a comprehensive inventory of proliferating signs of hyperturbulence is unnecessary sine the media report those signs so extensively n a global basis that further elaboration is needless. Suffice it to say that the extent of the turbulence is mirrored, for example, in wars and terrorist attacks; a national debt in the United States in excess of 37.2 percent of the gross national product; a technologically oriented, $7 billion a year business in pornography; and an increasing use of hightech devices in homes.

The sources of potential and already extant turbulence are virtually endless, but the small sample above will suffice as we turn attention to some of the ways in which the United States has become a micropermeated society to a degree beyond Orwellian imagination. The permeation, quite understandably, nurtures turbulence. For example:

1. The United States government embarked, as of 1983, on a program of computer expenditures that will total at least $28 billion by 1988. Recipients of an estimated one million computers include air traffic controllers, customs and passport personnel, and Social Security workers. Electronic mail networks link the white House to federal agencies. The Treasury Department receives global economic data via statelite. The Veterans Administration, Department of Agriculture, Department of Commerce, Library of Congress, National Library of Medicine, Internal Revenue Service, and FBI are more and more computer-based. The Food and Drug Administration has programmed a computer to react like a mouse.

2. Electronic invasion of privacy has become more and more common. Credit card "protection" bureaus now distribute comprehensive lists of credit cards to prospective customers. Via computers the bureaus patently have access to personal affairs, suggesting one more item on the roster of high-tech threats to our private lives.

3. The media, particularly television, permeate daily life. "Selected" news for the public consumption, diverse types of mind-numbling entertainment, and hidden or visible persuasion in many forms were deliberately or inadvertently made a part of our lives as Americans spent 1.5 billion hours per day viewing television in 1984.
4. The workplace has begun to be permeated by microelectronics. Some employees have been "telecommuting" and choosing their hours of work.

The roots of the sources of hyperturbulence and "present shock" are nourished by changes in the nature of change generated by high tech. It is highly important for educators to be aware of what has been wrought or facilitated by microelectronics.

Changes in the nature of change. For uncounted millennia, change has been more than glacially slow. Carl Sagan deftly points out that if all of time, sine time began, were squeezed into one year, then the single-cell life in the warm seas of past eons would not appear until September. The tread of the dinosaur would not shake the earth until the Christmas season, and early humans would not begin their long struggle for survival until 10 P.M. on new Year's eve. Furthermore, it would be 10:30 P.M. before our neolithic ancestors learned to chip tools from stones. The era for which history has preserved remembrance, occurs in the last few seconds prior to midnight in our "evolutionary year".

There have been crucial system-breaks in the pst, such as occurred at the end of Western Roman power in 476 A.D. But when Roman hegemony no longer existed from the Mediterranean Sea to Hadrinan's Wall, life-styles did not change dramatically. Spears and arrows continued to be used in battle. Fields wee tilled by oxen, and horses remained beasts of burden, There was little "techno-change" until the out, the world entered an ear off "technoshock". There was a dramatic change in the nature of change because of the creation and application of new technologies. In approximately fifty years, Platt tells us, there has been more acceleration in the rate of social evolution than in the previous six centuries. As an outcome, life on earth is at "the greatest turning point in four billion years". He goes on to say:

> The convergence of today's technological forces has produced a roaring waterfall of change. It leads onward to a great sea of new evolutionary possibilities on the earth and reaching into space. But right now we are in the torrent and our only hope is to work together with energy and intelligence if we are to come through successfully into that boundless ocean.

Hyperturbulence and holism. One of the lessons humans must learn-particularly educators working in administration and curriculum development-it that is a period of hyperturbulence, whatever educational changes are contemplated must be viewed holistically and systematically. We are now well into an epoch in which humans can never do one thing, an epoch in which any single action is certain to have consequences greater than the one (s) intended.

As was pointed out recently, the technological changes that occur (as in the various stages of computer development) have (a) intended (b) largely unexpected, and (c) unintended consequences. Microelectronic technologies, therefore, which have implications for education require that a holistic or "total picture" assessment be made of a proposed educational policy, program, or innovation.

The primary intent as television entered homes was to purvey education and entertainment. Representative of an unexpected outcome was the vast number of elementary school children who would sit up beyond midnight to watch late, late movies. An unintended impact was the decline of academic test scores which began in 1964 roughly twelve years after a cadre of 1952 kindergartens in the "TV generation" began taking the Scholastic Aptitude Test.

Patently, a holistic view must be taken in a given field of inquiry to contract the dangerous tunnel vision that could result from our failure to anticipate the unexpected and to avoid undesirable, unintended results that today's micromarvels may spawn.

Hardware and software: the "electronic twins"

Between the mid- 1940s and the mid-1970 most technological advances occurred in the area of computer hardware. Raw computer power was used to sell computers. What mattered was how many instructions a computer could handle, how much data it could store, and how fast it could process information. Dramatic reductions in the size and cost of computers, however, have made them increasingly attractive to the domestic, educational, and business markets. As a result, computers have now become largely on off-the-shelf commodity. They are no longer the specialized marvels of yesteryear. Indeed, they sometimes share such similar characteristics that in their marketing manufacturers often are forced to exaggerate the importance of the differences which presumably distinguish them.

Recently, the other "twin", software, has become more significant, especially to educators. The quality and diversity of software is of great significance in classroom instruction, curriculum development, and distance learning. It has meaning for aspects of administrative leadership, too, as noted elsewhere in this volume. This is why we have chosen the status of software art to conclude the first part of this chapter and also to serve as a bridge to our inquiry into general implications of microtechnologies for education.

Developments in software. Since 1980, many educators' interests have shifted from hardware to software. A decade or more ago, computers tended to be concentrated inside centralized data-processing areas where they were used primarily for clerical, accounting, and statistical purposes. Today, they are much more visible in living rooms, offices, classrooms, and work stations of all kinds. They handle a rapidly increasing range of tasks or functions including world processing, computer graphics, computer-assisted or computer-managed instruction, statistical analysis, financial data, inventory control, video games, and much more.

Computer owners initially tended to buy the computer first, then choose the software to go with it. Today, particularly in pursuing educational goals, it is advisable to examine the software one plans to use, then to select a computer than can run it efficiently. In addition, compatibility of software and hardware is also a problem, even with those systems purported to be compatible. "Compatibility" is governed not only by the capacities of hardware, but also by the way that the software is protected by the manufacturer. Therefore, the "friendliness" or compatibility of the system has also become an important consideration. It is a consumer-oriented property which is beginning to be a priority as software companies compete more vigorously with one another. Friendliness has particular implications for education, because it creates a decreasing need for users to learn programming. World-processing programs, spreadsheets, and database managers are emerging as the main programming "languages" of the 1980s.

As software became a more important concern of parents and teachers, computer programming ceased to be of secondary concern in our "Silicon Valleys". Many of the small companies of the 1970 have now become sizeable corporations. Hardware companies, even gaints such as Apple And IBM, are finding that they do not have sufficient resources to write all the programs needed for the overgrowing list of new uses for computers. Until recently, most software companies tended to specialize, but distinctions are becoming increasingly blurred. As the competition between software houses has grown and offerings have become more comprehensive, customers also have become more demanding. As a result, prices of programs have been reduced, customer feedback has been heeded, manuals have become more readable, and training programs have been made more widely available.

One improvement of particular importance in our schools is the recent development of flat television screens weighing less than two pounds and only three-quarters of an inch thick. Thus, true portability has become possible. Of all recent developments, however, none is more important than the evolution of integrated software for home and classroom. Integrated software replaces "stand-alone" grograms. One integrated program of particular merit for secondary and postsecondary education can do complex statistical projections on a spreadsheet, create graphics and charts from the database to illustrate the projections, enable the user to write a report merging the information, and, if need be, to transmit it by telephone to one of the several electronic universities that opened in 1984-85. Moreover, since integrated programs use the same commands and instructions, it is not now necessary to learn the intricacies of three, four, five, or more computer programs. Programs do not need to be changed, nor does information have to be re-entered. In the 1980s the task of using a single computer system for both teaching and administrative purposes has thus been simplified.

General implications of microtechnologies for education with emphasis on networking

In January, 1983, TIME broke a fifty-five-year precedent. For the first time a human being was replaced by computer as "Machine of the Year". "Yesterday's klutzy machines have become today's micromarvels", or so the editors of TIME advised their readers. And a machine became "personage" of the year.

The microchip moves in

The high-tech communications at Los Angeles were appreciably more extensive and impressive. The Games transported electronically to our homes were spread over 4,000 square miles, persons from fifty-one nations who spoke eighty-three languages were in the Olympic Community, and 17,000 terminals were brought in and placed at over sixty sites in order to insure comprehensive coverage.

Why do we begin this section of the chapter on the implications of microtechnologies by recounting the remarkable Olympic coverage in 1984? Because during the present decade the silicon ship, as it infuses us with information, has begun to approach and sometimes to transcend certain aspects of the input traditionally provided by schooling in the Unites States. As one outcome it is now increasingly necessary to consider as a single interwoven topic (a) the milieu created by the microchip and satellite and (b) the increasingly electronic surround provided for young learners by more and more schools and homes in America.

Documenting the extent and suddeness of the electronic explosion is report from Dataquest, a California-based research group, which reported that in 1980 twenty-four firms sold fewer than 750 thousand personal computers. By 1982, more than a hundred companies marketed approximately three million units.

The flood of current developments

Of the many electronic developments with a direct or indirect bearing on the teaching-learning process, educational networking apparently involves the largest cluster of challenges, advantages, and problems. Before examining the network concept in some depth, however, the fascinating complexity of a few of the inventions or events infiltrating complexity of a few of the inventions or events infiltrating human lives merits passing mention. They suggest the shape of things to come.

1. A nationwide portable cellular telephone service has become available as of 1984-85.
2. OMNI magazine recently published a short story written by a computer without human help.

3. At the Toko Auto Show a car which could respond to twenty-six preregistered voice commands was introduced.
4. In various sports, coaching by "biomechanical computer analysis" was developed.
5. A calculator wrist watch came on the market. It "reads" and records the numbers pressed on its glasscovered dial by a finger and then calculates as instructed. It also serves as a stopwatch and tells the hour.

At the same time, the world is becoming both a bigger and a smaller place. As we become submerged by information, the challenge is to extract knowledge from the flood of paper and electronic signals that bombard us. Information is transitory: knowledge is durable and self-propagating. The world is made of information, simple forms of which are matter and energy, but the biggest achievements of humankind are knowledge-based.

Services from microelectronic networks

The concept of the network as a means of keeping informed and as a means of coping with pyramidal bureaucracies or hierachies is an ancient one. The "Committees of Correspondence" in colonial times, "Old Boy hierarchies", and the "grapevine" are examples of traditional communications structures devised to keep ourselves informed.

In the realm of telecommunication information networks, there is a growing range and variety of electronic linkages, which are commonly known as databases.

Speed of growth. Microcomputer telecommunications seem fated to be the fastest growing segment of microchip-based industries. This because the proliferation of databases not only helps an individual to be informed but also to communicate, to engage in lifelong learning, and even to telecommute to work or to "tele-shop" rather than wait in line to be served at a store.

So rapidly has the home and office database grown in popularity that by 1985 there probably will be well over 350,000 subscribers to the various network services available from the "Big Three", and perhaps hundreds of other vendors. Just as ABC, CBS, and NBC continue to dominate television-although pressed in some areas by cable competitors-so three comparable "Big Three" purveyors of databases are dominant. In 1984, and in ascending order of clients served, the three were The source compuServe and the Dow-Jones News Retrieval Service.

The nature of available information services equipment. The gear needed for home, school, or corporation participation in microelectronic networks varies in price from a few hundred dollars to well over $10,000 depending on individual or institutional needs and aspirations. If one already owns a personal computer and has a touch-tone phone, the additional requirements are (a) a modem that transforms computer data into acoustical signals, or vice versa; (b) a software communication package; and (c) a communications interfacing component that physically coordinates sending and receiving information to an from other parts of the network via the modem and telephone circuit. If these items of equipment are available, the client can obtain series such as those mentioned in subsequent paragraphs by (a) dialing the local or WATS number for a given service and (b) providing the identification number and password. One is then "tuned in" or "on line" given data source. One need not be a programmer or understand a computer language to engage in networking.

Status of network services. Since there are dozens of vending companies and thousands of services offered through the various networks, a sampling of each must suffice. In addition to CompuServe, The Source, and Dow Jones News REtrieval, other representative on-line distributors of data, news, and educational information are; DIALOG, with Tens of millions of items in hundreds of databases; Electronic Information Exchange System (EIES); MINET (Medical Information Network) sponsored by the American Medical Association; News net, producer of electronic newsletters; Bibliographic Retrieval Service (BRS), emphasizing scientific data; Mead Data Control, with a huge law library services and the exclusive rights to the complete text of the New Your Times; Computer Bulletin Boards (CBBs) operated by hobbyists for like-interest groups.

Various networks, such as those listed above, provide a growing list of services. For example, COMP-U-STORE of Stamford, Connecticut, purveys over 60,000 products; Tradenet permits persons "to network" barter deals; and a Canadian firm will lease a database dealing with demographies and marketing prospects in a given geographical area. Information on Demand (IOD) Specializes in Exotic questions and will even translate technical Japanese or Chinese charactrers into other written languages.

Networks and education. The extent to which networking is contributing to education is substantial. Compuserve has arranged an advisory service in which faculty members from between 200 and 3000 secondary schools provide on-line advice regarding such matters as preparing for SAT's or selecting a compatible university. The constantly updated research-retrieval information available through DIALOG and the opportunity for students to request reference materials on wide variety of topics from librarians are of obvious value. Two rival computer networks in Britain now make it possible to link all of that country's 6,500 secondary schools. Schools will be able to "network" with other schools and to interact with business and industry. It is envisaged, for instance, that employers will relay career information and job applications directly to terminals in the schools. Students will complete the application forms on the terminals in the schools and "return" them instantly via computer mail services.

Electronic on -screen reference books, updated from day to day, also are available. As of mid-1984, on two networks there were around 90,000 subscribers resting the idea of a network encyclopedia and, at present, are also exploring other electronic alternatives, Some limited and controlled experiments had been undertaken by 1983-84 in schools in the United States in an effort to improve basic reading skills by means of computers.

Teleconference networking and electronic mail also are beginning to be used in education.

Teleconference networking and electronic mail also are beginning to be used in education. Teleconferencing is similar to electronic mail in that it transmits data, audio and video, from one location to another, but interactively. In time communication within or between school systems seems likely. There is ample precedent in the business community. By mid-1984 a company making electronic instruments, Hewlett-Packard, was exchanging some 100,000 electronic messages daily with 15,000 employees in fifty locations around the globe.

Educators within larger cities, or when separated by thousands of miles, can exchange information. For instance, in a "wired" school a teacher, principal, or nurse can type a note to a school physician on a computer and describe the symptoms of a child suddenly taken ill. Return advice can be expected in a matter of a minute or two. "Voicemail" systems, where spoken messages are recorded via telephone-computer units, also are in their early stages.

The computer: an educational partner?

If we are to accept views expressed in much of the

literature we have reviewed in preparing this chapter, it is likely that in the next two decades microelectronics and network databases will virtually become educators' partners in the classroom, office, and laboratory. If this is the case, we will need to answer with prudence, reasoned by Chorover: How will microcomputers and associated microelectronic technologies affect the form and content of education? What effect will their introduction have on the personal and professional lives of students, teachers, and administrators? How will it effect relationships, as well as the quality of the interactions, between the individuals and groups of people involved in the educational process? We now consider each of these queries.

Changing form an curriculum content. Here. educators confront the basic challenge of the impact of microelectronics on the curriculum and instruction. It seems likely, as computers become even more sophisticated, and as they retrieve information even more efficiently, that there will be not a decreasing but an increasing need for reading, speaking, and writing skills. There also seems certain to be a need for expanded knowledge with respect to the content and application of the subject matter of the natural and social sciences. The computer and networks purvey information; they do not dispense the ability to understand or interpret this input. As a result of increased input, the meaning of meaning needs to be emphasized. This includes helping young learners to recognize flawed communication, trival or "junk" communication, manipulated news, and the ways in which those forms of communication, including books and journals, that bring wisdom can best be exploited.

In short, redesign of the curriculum must eventuate in the widespread literacy-based know-how that is essential in a society with a high "survival quotient". Furthermore, even the presumed "great leap" that the artificial intelligence of fifth-generation computers may initiate will demand more, rather than less, knowledge and wisdom of humans. The importance of judgment, perception and intuition in both teaching and learning is likely to increases as computerized knowledge systems assume more of the burdens of memorization, retrieval, and analysis.

Changing personal professional roles: Students, teachers, administrators. Not only will the personal and educational roles and young learners undergo mutations in coming decades; mature and senior learners and professional educators can anticipate new experiences for the new epoch.

Various experiences and exposures are suggested for administrators and teachers. The following sampling of possible innovations in our schools merits particular attention not just in view of the revolutionary developments we have already described but because of their implications for many members of the community.

1. A basic knowledge of the increasing complexity

and versatility of the computer and of the overall microelectronic milieu should be acquired. Special heed must be given to the growing range and variety of network input for both faculty and students at home as well as at school. As Neil postman has pointed out, by 1980 students who were graduated from high schools in the United States had spent some 15 or 16 thousand hours watching television, versus the 12 thousand hours they spent in elementary and secondary classrooms. The computer in the home, including videogames, is increasing the discrepancy. Clearly, ways of monitoring and utilizing the total electronic surround must become a greater part of the preparation of teachers and adult lifelong learning skills, and the use of access to networks need to follow new paths. Technological unemployment created by increased robotization lends an increasing urgency for retrofitting or retraining the jobless.

2. First-hand acquaintance with the range and variety of software available for elementary and secondary pupils and adults is needed. Also, the adaptability of hardware to proliferating information on networks must constantly be reviewed by teachers and, as appropriate, shared with learners.

3. Course work in administration at both the undergraduate and graduate levels should include a study of (a) the basic nature of the skills of computer operation plus some "hands

on" contacts; (b) an introduction to curriculum planning that anticipates and is derived from developments that are shaping the future; and (c) improved and increased input from arts and science college courses dealing with megatrends that are shaping society. Continuing "literacy upgrading", including basic skills testing, is essential in all course work.

4. Because of the rapidity of change in microelectronics, continuing "competency updates" through short-term workshops and conferences should be sponsored at the university level for school employees and parents.
5. Content of course syllabi and of policy books in such areas as school plant, law, finance, public relations, and basic administration should be checked periodically by the school administration and faculty to help insure that the implications of current microelectronic developments are included and emerging developments anticipated.
6. When feasible, sabbaticals for administrators and teachers, or at least short-term residencies, should be arranged so that participants have access to electronically equipped "vanguard" schools or university computer centers.
7. Finally, teaches and administrators should be helped to understand that their teaching and leadership potential can be threatened and

perhaps sharply diminished if they allow themselves to become dependent on (a) "micro-wise" assistants of (b) too dependent on a computer system as a substitute for their own personal critical thinking.

Human relations in educational processes. In the emerging electronic educational realms, one short statement has acquired greatly enhanced significance; Carefully planned teamwork and cooperation have never been more vital than they will be in the future.

Successful teamwork already is coming into being among parents and other community residents, students, teachers, administrators, school boards, and trustees because of the tremendously versatile silicon chip. The opportunity for human beings to work together and to live well with their microbiotechnological creations has never been greater, and never has it been fraught with greater potential peril in a time of ecological and nuclear dangers.

As we acquire the higher skills of successful interaction, our success as teamworkers will be greater as we recognize that there are multiple facets of the learners' intelligence in the widest sense of the term. We have tended to stress and to test verbal and mathematical skills. Far less has been done to polish the artistic, musical, and kinesthetic forms of intelligence. By and large interpersonal or social intelligence skill in working with others-and interpersonal or self-knowledge insights have often been taken for granted. They now need careful cultivation.

A part of successful human relations in the educational world of tomorrow will involve shaping a wide range of talents to strengthen the faculty and to obtain the best of the varied social and intellectual skills that each member possesses.

Computer caveats and cautions

Although the prospects for the positive application of microelectronics in education are bright, a few caveats and cautions need to be kept in mind.

The EMP., first society and its schools need to preserve some effective back-up strategies because one single nuclear blast would be likely to give off an electromagnetic pulse (EMP) that could lobotomize computers along with other circuitry. The EMP phenomenon, which travels with the speed of light, is an intense burst of magnetic energy that burns out electrical systems. A nuclear bomb exploded 250 miles above a midwestern state presumably would envelop the United States with EMP which has peak fields of 50,000 volts per meter-probably enough to make most of our power and communications systems useless-including those operated by the military.

Since EMP was identified as a threat in 1962, billion s of dollars have been spent by the military in a unsuccessful effort to safeguard our electronic gear. The maintenance of freedom from overdependence on sophisticated microelectronic communication systems seems crucial.

Electronic cocoons. A second caveat or caution pertains to social and intellectual development.

We should not bring up a generation of computer buffs and hackers to whom their "friendly" computer has become more important than human friends. Social group situations must not be replaced by electronic cocoons, places in which to retreat from reality.

In fairness, it also should be noted that computers can be "fun chums" because of the interesting electronic games that are available. The problem is to help young people benefit intellectually and improve their physical coordination without becoming "video junkies" frequenting arcades and feeding billions of quarters into coin slots.

Scholars' warnings. Highly respected scholars have in recent years voiced concerns about the computer as a threat to thinking. Of particular interest is the recent comment made by Professor Joseph Weizenbaum of the Massachusetts Institute of Technology who invented the Eliza computer program and is an authority on artificial intelligence. In an interview for Le Nouvel Observateur he was asked, "do you think, then, that France is making a mistake by trying to put computers in everyone's hands?"

Weizenbaum If that is what France is doing, then, yes, it's making a mistake. The temptation to send in computers wherever there is a problem area, be it medicine, education, or whatever, usually creates the impression that grievous deficiencies are being corrected... But often its principles effect is to push problems even further into obscurity-to avoid confrontation with the need for fundamentally critical thinking.

'All the computers in the world won't help you if your unexamined and unconscious assumptions on the nature of reality are simply wrong in their basic conception. All the computers can do is to help you to be stupid in an expensive fashion.

Concluding comment

The metaphor of a series of wages washing over education is particularly useful in the context of microelectronic technologies. Just as most wages develop in an area for removed from the shoreline on which they break, so much of the original interest in the potentialities of the micro-age began as an array of seemingly unrelated innovations at least partly removed from the school environment. Only since the mid-1970s has the development of relatively inexpensive microcomputers-machines capable of an entertainment function as well as more serious uses-captured the attention of both children and adults. As of the mid-1980s, as noted earlier, the computer is rapidly becoming the symbol of a new technologically permeated society.

Useful in themselves as free-standing decides, whether for instruction, home study, or for administration, much of the potential of the microcomputer is yet to be realized. As microcomputers become even more adequately "networked", they seem certain to become part of a total information-knowledge communication system, involving speech, video, and print. At the local, regional, national, or international level, diverse technological components are now able to interface with each other. This is the result of the recent convergence of the computer and related microelectronic communications technologies. The synergism that has resulted is now guiding educators into a knowledge-based communications system which is different in character and kind from the more traditional technologies involved in the educational practices of yesteryear.

The full implications of the labyrinthine microelectronic technologies associated with extended networks, however, have only begun to be experienced. The advent of fifth-generation computer systems that can think and may well be able to reason could make possible in the next two decades the development of a total teaching-learning system which is extraordinarily efficient and effective. Although some would view such a system as potentially dehumanizing, this is not necessarily so. A computerized information-communications system, in itself, is inherently neither good nor bad, but it is powerful. What makes it good or bad is how we learn to use to, how intelligently we apply our skills as thinking people.

As Hamlet reminds us, "There is nothing either good or bad, but thinking makes it so". Microtechnologies will be "good" or "bad" to the degree that we use them with wisdom or folly in education and the wider society. In this sense, electronic microbiotechnologies seem likely to provide a test for humankind. As Turkle suggests, individuals can use computer systems to establish personal identity, to gain self-awareness, to achieve a feeling of mastery over their present lives, and to direct their alternative futures.

The newly developed body of microelectronic resources epitomized by the computer has an imposing array of brilliant potential solutions for a number of our personal-social problems. it is up to us, as educators, to establish priorities as we address the problems of effective teaching and learning. In this way, we will best be able to utilize our newest resources to prepare learners of all ages for successful living in the new millennium which is close at hand.

8 Computer-Related Learning in Vocational Education

There is by now no doubt that computers and related technologies have had, and will continue to have, for far-reaching effects on the United States and the world economy and employment. There is a broad range of views in the scholarly literature and popular press about the nature and extent of these effects. Despite a rapidly changing present and an increasingly uncertain future, however, vocational educators must provide their students with the opportunity to acquire skills, knowledge, and attitudes needed in order to survive and thrive in what is often called the "information society".

Because of the highly visible and influential roles of computers and related technology in the post industrial economy and society, considerable attention is currently being paid to the concept of computer literacy in preparing students for work.

The purpose of this chapter is to assist educators, leaders in industry, and government officials to identify needs and directions for computer-related learning in vocational education. The following questionnaire addressed:

1. How important are computer-related skills and knowledge in preparing students for the workplaces of the information society?
2. What computer-related skills and knowledge are or will be needed in sample occupations?
3. What needs to be done to make vocational education programs more responsive to students' career and vocational needs, give the changing workplace and occupational structures?

Computer-related need in vocational education should be derivable from systematic analyses of tasks performed in the occupations addressed by particular vocational education programs. In the classical approach to instructional systems development, one analyzes the job tasks to be performed and then derives requirements for skill and knowledge requirements are then transformed into instructional objectives.

In preparing this chapter, my initial intent was (a) to select a sample of three occupational areas; (b) to gather all available job/task inventories for those areas; (c) to extract all computer-related tasks from these inventories and analyze them for their implications for computer-related skill and knowledge needed for those jobs; and (d) to compare these requirements with existing vocational education curricula in these occupational areas and to identify areas needing revision or improvement. The methodology was unsuccessful because currently available job/task inventories do not reject computer-related tasks, computer-based methods, or changing job descriptions. It became apparent that the methods, or changing job descriptions. It became apparent that the methods and procedures currently employed for developing and disseminating job/risk inventories are inadequate for handling the rapid pace of technological change in america's workplaces. A revised approach was to take a broader look at the impact of technology on change in the economy and occupational structures in the United States and to take a long-range look at the implications of these changes on requirements for vocational education objectives and programs. Computer-related needs in the three sample occupation areas were then analyzed in the context of this broader view.

What is vocational education?

Vocational education is defined in the Education Amendments of 1976 as "organized programs which are directly related to the preparation of individuals for paid or unpaid employment, or for additional preparation for a career requiring other than a baccalaureate or advanced degree".

Vocational education provides occupational training to millions of people in many different types of educational institutions across the United States. In 1980-81, the National Centre for Education Statistics estimated that 16.9 million people were enrolled in vocational education programs supported in part by the vocational Education Act of 1963 as amended. This figure does not include students enrolled in the many institutions that are privately controlled. Including those students raises the total to nearly 19 million. However, information on students in programs not supported by the vocational Education Act is sparse and is not included in our discussion.

Of the 16.9 million vocational students, about 5.8 million were enrolled in programs designed to train individuals for specific occupations. Occupationally specific programs are offered in grades eleven and twelve as well as in postsecondary and adult education schools.

The vocational education programs supported with federal funds cover education in the following categories identified by the U.S. Department of Education's National Occupational Information Coordinating Committee: agriculture/agribusiness and natural resources, business and office occupations, health occupations, home economics, marketing and distribution, technical occupations, and the trade and industrial occupations. Industrial arts, which is not included in the list, is not an occupationally specific program but includes courses surveying occupations as well as metal working and woodworking.

The two most popular programs are business and office programs and trade and industrial programs, in which a total of more than 60 percent of all vocational education students are enrolled. This pair of programs dominates enrollments at all levels.

The changing workplace

Lacking a clear vision of the workplace of tomorrow, educators and their students could well waste billions of dollars and person-years in counterproductive efforts to acquire irrelevant or low-priority skills and knowledge. It is impossible to predict with certainty with the occupational structures will be in twenty or thirty years, much less what the specific skill and knowledge requirements of those jobs will be.

Yet the purpose of "computer literacy" especially in vocational education, is to prepare young people for work in the information-rich, highly computerized offices, homes, farms, and factories of the future. This, computer literacy is a high risk educational venture. It is high risk both because of the uncertain payoff in terms of relevance to tomorrow's jobs and because of the high costs associated with acquisition of computing equipment and provision of teacher training programs needed for adequate computer literacy curricula.

Changing technology creates dilemmas

It has been pointed out that "productive members of society will increasingly be expected to modify, upgrade, and update their knowledge and skills in response to a pace of technological change at least as rapid as occurred during the great industrialization of America a century ago... Given the uncertainty regarding the skill requirements of the economy, it is essential that the education of America's as necessary to these changing requirements."

The vocational education pattern in the past has been to institute computer-related programs of study that are oriented toward technology from the preceding generation of computers. In the early 1970s, computer-related curricula were oriented toward batch processing and keypunching, while the technology was moving toward interactive time-sharing systems. In the mid-1970s, when microcomputers were appearing on the market, educational programs were being upgraded to reflect the advent of time sharing. In the late 1970s and early 1980s, when the availability of general purpose applications programs were rendering programming skills obsolete for most computer users, many schools began instituting courses to teach all students programming on microcomputers. New that technological advances are rendering many data-entry specialist jobs obsolete, some schools are instituting training in data entry. Now that computer-based work stations in business offices are integrating word-processing, data-processing, and communications functions, some schools are instituting training for dedicated word-processing machines and word-processing specialist jobs.

How serious a problem is rapid change in technology for teachers and students in vocational education courses of study? The answer depends entirely on the goals and objectives of the courses. If the students are acquiring fundamental concepts and skills in information handling and problem solving, then the characteristics and limitations of the particular machines and methods they are using are more or less incidental. If, on the other hand, students are merely being *trained* in narrow skills of operation of a particular device or program, then the consequences of using obsolete or nearly obsolete equipment are very serious.

Changing technology will be a fact of life in all workplaces for the foreseeable future. Learning to use new machines and new kinds of machines will be a part of every job. Even more significantly, learning new ways of organizing and managing information will be a continuing process for everyone. Consider, for example, the career of a hypothetical secretary over the past five years. She may have begun performing a wise variety of tasks for her employer. including typing on a typewriter. Then the organization set up a centralized word-processing centre, and she was transferred there, to specialize in operating a new dedicated word processor. After a year, the company reorganized and she was transferred to another division where a different kind of word processor communicated with an office data-processing machine. Now the company has acquired general purpose personal computers, and she is learning to use not only a word-processing program for the personal computer but an electronic spreadsheet, a database management program, and communications programs. She is setting up procedures for transferring data from the spreadsheet to the word-processing program and is organizing the disk-file library for her group.

Viewed in the context of this career path, it would appear to make little difference what particular equipment was used or what specific skills she learned in her vocational education program in school. What could make a difference in her ability to adapt successfully and productively to new job requirements, however, would be the skills, knowledge, and attitudes related to learning new methods of handling information, developing procedures, learning how to learn about new machines, and collaborating with co-workers in problem-solving situations.

The uncertain impact of automation on employment and job skills

There is a broad range of views in the scholarly literature and popular press about the nature and extent of the effects of computer-based automation on he united States economy, on employment, and on job skills. At one extreme it is claimed that the future will require much less skilled workforce. At the other extreme it is said that the future will require a more highly skilled and technologically oriented workforce.

The less-skill perspective. The first scenario of technology's impact on future job skills is that, essentially, "machines will do it all". This view implies that many human tasks will be simplified as machines perform the majority of complex operations.

Levin and Rumberger's widely quoted thesis is that "the expansion of the lowest skilled jobs in the American economy will vastly outstrip the growth of high technology ones; and the proliferation of high technology industries and their products is far more likely to reduce the skill requirements of jobs in the U.S. economy than to upgrade them." These authors address two aspects of the changing workforce: the nature of future employment growth and the impact of technology on existing jobs.

With regard to future employment growth, Levin and Rumberger rely heavily on U.S. Department of Labour predictions that the largest increases in *new* openings in the 1980s will be in low-skill jobs: janitors, nurses' aides, salesclerks, cashiers, and waiters and waitresses. These predictions differ from those that look at the numbers of annual job openings.

With regard to the impact of technology on existing jobs, Levin and Rumberger base their analysis on analogy with the industrial revolution. Mechanization was applied in the workplace in such a manner as to fragment work tasks into simplified operations that required few skills to perform. Basing their reasoning on past experience in industrialization, they conclude that "future technologies will further simplify and routinize work tasks and reduce opportunities for worker individuality and judgment".

The more-skill perspective. Most analysts disagree with Levin and Rumberger's analysis. For example, Leontief and Duchin's analysis results sin a nearly opposite conclusion. They developed an input-output model of the United

States economy, using four different scenarios of the progressive introduction of computers and various forms of computer-based automation into eighty-nine individual industries. Their model spells out in great detail the probable effects of these technological changes on outputs and inputs of all goods and services and in particular on the demand for labour services in fifty-three different occupations. they find, for example, that "the intensive use of automation over the next twenty years... will involve a significant increase in professionals as a proportion of the labour force and a steep decline in the relative number of clerical workers."

A report of the Education Commission of the States agrees with our concern that "by examining the skills needed in tomorrow's labour force we can better prepare workers for the changing conditions they will encounter." The report points out that other factors besides breakthroughs in technology are significantly related to economic growth. these other factors are "advances in new knowledge and increased education levels of the work force." The report states that occupational growth throughout the 1980s is projected to expand most rapidly in the higher-skilled, technical occupations. "Tomorrow's workers will likely need improved skills in the selection and communication of information. Many of today's skills considered to be of a 'higher' level are the potential basic skills of tomorrow."

According to the Commission's report, these skills include evaluation and analysis skills, critical thinking, problem-solving strategies, organization and reference skills, synthesis, application, creativity, decision making given incomplete information, and communication skills though a variety of modes.

A third view: transformation. Part of the reason for the discrepancies in views of the future may be that as a society we are in a period of transformation or paradigm shifts as characterized by such writers as Masuda, Toffler, and Ferguson. Toffler's view is that in the industrial age the "workers" were *trained* to perform repetitive tasks requiring varying degrees of skill. The "thinkers" were *educated* to solve problems, make decisions, and manage workers and information. If on imposes this industrial age paradigm on lowered skill requirements for the "workers". A frequently cited example is Levin's claim that the use of word processors reduces the skill requirements for typists. This kind of thinking is often reported in the public media.

The industrial age paradigm was characterized succinctly in Boyer's discussion of the tracking of students into "academic" and "nonacademic" paths: "Students are divided between those who think and those who work, when, in fact, life for all of us is a blend of both." If one applies this "working and thinking" paradigm to the example cited earlier of the claim of reduced skill requirements for typists using word processors, one makes a different interpretation. For example, a "thinker" using a word processor may be performing operations and making decisions that we used to think required higher-order skills, such as planning the organization of document files, designing file templates for repetitive correspondence, writing procedures using variables, programming keyboard macros, developing procedures for integrating data files with documents, selecting appropriate typestyles and document formats, and developing a library of standardized templates. Form this point of view, the person who is typing with a word processor is relieved of lower-level skill requirements such as details of formatting and the checking of spelling and is freed to attend to higher-level information handling concerns.

In my view, it is the "worker" versus "thinker" kind of paradigm that leads such analysts as Levin and Rumberger to imagine that computer-based technology will necessarily result in the need for a less skilled workforce. They refer to the ways in which industrialization resulted in specialization and lowered skill requirements on the part of workers and imagine that the same trends will continue with computer-based automation. Their analysis does not take into account the fact that computers can be used to extend the human intellect, thereby allowing humans to be more creative and powerful problem solvers. By participating in the process of creating knowledge, the human adds value to the product or service involved, thereby contributing to the productivity of the overall information-based economy.

Technology-related occupations in vocational education

Traditionally, there computer-related skills and knowledge that have been taught in vocational education have been in the occupational areas of computer operation and data entry clerk. For several years concerns have been voiced about the increasing supply of computer operators and data entry clerks from vocational education programs and the dwindling number of available positions. Furthermore, the people being employed are better educated and are filling more skilled positions.

A 1975 survey noted that the number of graduates from the postsecondary vocational and associate level programs might soon exceed the number in the labour market. This report assumed that associated degree institutions were training students primarily for data entry operators and clerical data processing positions.

In commenting on institutional resources for computing, alcorn stated:

The makeup of the staff of the computer installations is changing toward a higher percentage of analysts and programmers and a lower percentage of operators, toward more full-time and less part-time employees, and toward a slightly better educated staff."

Schools that understood changes in occupations attempted to shift their emphasis to "newer" computer-based jobs and away from heavy emphasis on computer-operator and data entry positions. Though they continued to offer these courses, many programs were expanding their vision.

The traditional vocational education programs in computer operations and data entry are slowly being replaced by programs in the so-called "Emerging" high-tech occupations such as robotics technician, communications specialist, and computer-assisted design/computer-assisted manufacturing technicians.

By 1990, 80,000 to 100,000 will be in use, according to Walter Wiesel, president of Robot Institute of America, a trade association, and of PRAB Robots, a manufacturing firm. Other figures regarding the robotic revolution are more conservatives. Allan Hunt of the Upjohn institute predicts that 50,000 to 100,000 robots will be is use. But he also warns that over half the jobs created by robotics will require two or more years of college-level training. Wiesel agrees with Hunt's assessment on the amount of training necessary for robotic technicians. He says the typical worker in this area will be a person who "understands what the arm is supposed to operate like at the job site". Table displays the types of jobs expected to be created by advancements in robotics.

Direct job creation in U.S. due to robotics, by occupations, 1990

	Employment Range of Estimate	
Occupation	*Law*	*High*
Engineers	4,636	3,272
Robotics technicians	12,284	24,568
Other engineering technicians	664	1,328

Cont...

All other professional and technical workers	936	1,871
Managers, officials, proprietors	1,583	3,166
Sales workers	581	1,162
Clerical workers	2,908	5,817
Skilled craft and related workers	2,163	4,326
Semiskilled metal working operators	2,153	4,306
Assemblers and all other operatives	3,763	7,526
Service workers	138	276
Labourers	279	558
Total	32,088	64,176

Job/task inventories as bases for new requirements in vocational programs

It has been assumed by training developers that the design of effective educational and training programs must be founded on detailed and systematic analysis of the task to be performed on the job. Conducting empirical studies of tasks performed by workers in a particular job category is a costly undertaking, usually beyond the resources of an individual school. Therefore, regional and national centres and consortia have been established, to provide job/task inventories and job-relevant catalogues of performance objectives, criterion-references measures, and performance guides.

The High Technology Education Project of the Office for rEsearch in High Technology education at the University of Tennessee attempted to obtain all available job/task inventories for the three selected occupational areas from a wide variety of such centres throughout the United States. Secretarial occupations represent the largest number of annual job openings nationally. Drafting is being radically affected by computer-aided design and drafting systems. Because computer applications in accounting are older than computer applications in any other field of endeavour, dating back to the 1950s at least, it was expected that accounting occupations would provide insight into how technology is integrated into traditional occupations.

For our purposes in this chapter we examined available job/task inventories in order to (a) find out the computer-related skills and knowledge needed by workers in the sampling of occupation areas, (b) discover computer-related skill s and knowledge that are common across occupations, and (c) to find out what information is available to vocational curriculum developers and teachers regarding the computer-related skills and knowledge needed by their students.

From the stand-point of identifying computer-related tasks, skills, and knowledge, the inventories examined were essentially useless. Even job/task catalogues published as recently as 1983 included few or no computer-related task. Nearly all the secretarial job/task inventories ignored the use of word processes and other kinds of programs on general purpose computers in an office setting. The same is true of th bookkeeping and accounting inventories. In drafting, few inventories were available; those that were available made no mention of the use of computer-aided design and graphics programs.

The one task listing that does identify several computer-related tasks illustrates a major weakness in inventories of the kind reviewed here. In that document computer-related tasks are described almost solely in behavioural terms. The cognitive components of such a task are far more important from any education or training stand-point than the far more important from any educational or training stand-point than the behavioural manipulation of the keys. In reading the task lists, one gets the impression that the one thing workers do not do is think. Rarely in the task lists do they make decisions, analyze information, solve problems, apply principles, and make trade-offs.

Techniques for analyzing tasks for their cognitive components are in their infancy. At the least, however, it would be useful for developing curricula if job/task analyses states the purpose of goals or a task from the viewpoint of the task performer. Such information would be useful in grouping related tasks for instructional analysis and sequencing of instruction. For example, in word processing, statements such is "embeds control characters into text strings" are less useful than statements that reveal the underlying purpose of the operations. To continue with the previous example, the person might be embedding the control characters for such purposes as specifying or modifying document or page formats, documenting procedure, or reorganizing document content. Such purpose are accomplished through different behavioural operations on different machines or software. A person attempting to become computer-literate needs to develop a cognitive framework that enables his or her to understand basic purposes and functions and transfer these understandings across different machine environments.

The present system of creating and updating job/task inventories is of little value as a basis for developing up-to-date curricula or even identifying task, skills, an knowledge needed in workplaces that are in a continual state of change with respect to applications of technology. The inventory procedure takes several years for gathering date, it relies on survey responses from job incumbents in representative firms. The methodology described in the inventory documents does not attempt to take into account the fact that jobs are changing .

Requirements for secretarial occupations

To provide an example of the implications of the changing workplace for vocational education, the following section discusses secretarial occupations. Similar considerations apply to other office occupations such as accounting and bookkeeping. In the area of drafting, even more extensive changes are occurring than in the secretarial example, due to the increasing us of computer-aided design, drafting, and engineering systems.

As noted previously, secretarial jobs will account for th largest number of annual job openings during the 1980s. For perspective, compare the 305,000 projected annual openings for secretaries with the estimated range of 12,000 to 24,0000 jobs for robotics technicians in 1990. Secretarial training programs are one of the most successful vocational education programs, in terms of employment results. These two factors justify paying attention to the continual improvement and modernization of secretarial programs in vocational education.

Methods and systems for handling information in offices continue to change due to continuing improvements and reductions in cost for computer-and communications-based technologies. Relationships among various organizational groups and subsystems in even small businesses are being rethought due to chages in the technology available for gathering, storing, organizing, retrieving, and communicating information. For example, five or ten years ago word professing machines were special purpose devices costing tens of thousands of dollars and were considered to require "word processing specialists" to operate. Now, word processing programs are available at a cost of $50 to $400, and they operate on general purpose desktop computers at any desk where there is an electronical outlet. A business person who pays to little for a word processor does not expect to have to capacity is an everyday tool of anyone in an office who needs to produce written documents. one should not expect to have to take a specialist program of studies in word processing to learn to use word processors. Learning to use word processors should be a normal part of secretarial programs in vocational education.

Changes in information-handling systems in offices

A wide variety of data-management, data-processing, communications, and other functions can easily be performed by nonspecialists using the general purpose computer that is the heart of the modern office workstation. This allows for greater integration of various information-handling functions than has been the case in the past. More importantly, it means continual changes in information-handling systems for the foreseeable future. Implications for vocational education of this trend toward integrated work situations are several. First, narrow specialist training in dedicated word-processor operations is less valuable in the job market than general information-processing skills. Second, the kinds of applications software a secretary needs to operate are changing. Communications, spreadsheets, databases, and accounting programs are just as important tools for the workstation as are word processors.

Third, the integration of the workstation allows for more integration of the functions of information processing. Therefore one can expect less, rather than more, specialization of office jobs. An executive who uses spreadsheets for modelling and decision making, databases for information retrieval, and word processing for preparing reports and correspondence does not want to have a separate secretary or technician to operate each separate program. The secretary or whatever the person is called must be equally comfortable with typing documents, entering formulas for spreadsheet computations, or requesting sorts from the data management program.

Most experts foresee the need for secretarial personnel to have higher-level skills and greater adaptability than in the past. Nearly all of the analyses reviewed for the present study predict that secretarial jobs will continue to require more analytic abilities, greater adaptability, and greater skills in decision making, communications, and interpersonal relations. Understanding of basic concepts of systems analysis, data processing, the telecommunications is seen as necessary in support of this increased adaptability. A fairly extreme version of this point of view was expressed by Stewart:

> The day may not be too far off when secretarial jobs will require a master's degree in business administration and be regarded as an entry-level step into management. There will be more creative-type positions, few dog-work-type tasks and there will be far more tasks.

Given the inescapable conclusion that business offices will continue to change in the nature of computer-based equipment and in the methods of handling information, what is the most important computer-related skill or knowledge a person preparing to be a secretary could have? Clearly, one cannot point to any given device or program of today and say: "This is the kind of machine of must be trained to operate". Even the more generic skill of keyboarding is suspect in a world where voice input, optical scan input, and direct computer-to-computer transfer of data could reduce keyboarding demands overnight.

The most useful computer-related idea that a secretary could develop is that he or she be able to learn the capabilities, limitations, functions, and operations of any particular computer-based systems when the need arises to do so. The development of this concept, and the related attitude of confidence, can be encouraged by an educational environment that expects students to learn how to learn. For example, students learning to operate an unfamiliar word-processing program would not be taught step-step specific procedures of operation. Rather, they would be introduced to the basic functions of the program and would be provided with a use's manual and/or the on-line helps and menus built into the program. They would be asked to solve problems and accomplish tasks to progressive levels of complexity. Working independently or in small groups, students would develop confidence and skill in using available information to teach themselves how to solve problems and accomplish new tasks. REading, writing, oral communications, procedural thinking, keyboarding, familiarity with characteristics of electronic storage media, and a minimal computer-related vocabulary are prerequisite to success in such problem-solving and independent-learning tasks.

The kinds of programs secretarial students need to learn how to use include word processors and associated utilities such as spelling an grammar checkers, electronic spreadsheets, data-management programs, graphics programs, and communications programs. Since the way in which such programs actually operate is constantly changing it is important for students to learn not only the specifics of using a particular program. They need to learn the basic information-handling functions tha such programs can perform, their capacities, and their limitations.

The status of computer literacy in vocational education

If one defines computer literacy in functional way, that is, whatever a person needs to be able to do with computer in order to function effectively in a particular role, then one would expect to see the integration of computer-related tools, methods, and concepts into the curriculum in nearly every integration would be reflected in some of the following ways:

1. Job and task inventories for the office and industrial occupations would reflect the computer-related and information-handling task performed and skills and knowledge required in those occupations.
2. State and local education agencies would be providing guidance on computer-literacy needs in vocational education.
3. Curriculum guides for occupational programs would reflect skills and knowledge needed in

relation to technology and information handling.

4. Vocational education conferences would contain sessions and papers on topics related to the integration of computer-related skills into various vocational education courses.
5. Secondary schools would be sponsoring or conducting in service workshops for vocational education teachers, to increase their computer-related skills.
6. Teacher training institutions would be preparing new vocational education teachers to use computer-based tools methods, and media in their instructional programs.
7. Textbooks and other learning materials used in vocational education would incorporate computer-based methods and materials.
8. Software and educational publishers seeing a market in vocational education for software designed for vocational education curricula, would be offering computer programs to fit into the various curriculum areas.

A survey of the above indicators would be likely to yield useful insights on change processes in vocational education. Although a systematic survey of these indicators in beyond the scope of the present chapter, the following comments on each may be helpful.

State and local education agencies. According to an October 1984 survey of state education agencies, twenty states has by then passed laws requiring or recommending some form of computer-literacy instruction in their K-12 schools. Many states' guidelines has moved in the direction of integrating computer-related skills and knowledge into the traditional courses. Although few of these state directives and guidelines relate specifically to vocational education, they have strong implications for the computer-related skills that can be expected on the part of students entering vocational education programs.

The California State Department of Education Office of Vocational Education has prepared a draft for a computer literacy guide for business education that addresses three levels of computer literacy:awareness, operations, and competence. The California competence objectives illustrate the idea that students need to learn not just rote procedures, but rather how to apply computer-based tools to the tasks of their jobs.

In 1983, Kapp and Knickerbocker surveyed state directors of vocational education to determine whether microcomputers were being purchased for use in vocational education in their states, how the computers were being used, and the percentage of teachers using microcimputers. They found that 35 per cent of the junior and senior high schools has purchased more than fifty micro-cimputers, although it is unclear whether all of these were for vocational education. Ninety-six percent of the respondents said that the most frequent use was for word processing. Seventy-eight percent of the respondents said that fewer than 50 percent of their teachers were using microcimputers.

Curriculum guidelines. Some recent local and regional curriculum guidelines for the areas of occupations, drafting, and accounting occupations were reviewed for this chapter. Although many of the programs reviewed included computer-related competencies or topics, these topics were usually not integrated into the regular curriculum but rather were tacked on as separate courses in computers or information processing. It must be emphasized, however, that the resources for the present chapter precluded systematic evaluation of published curriculum guides.

Conferences. The topic of computer-related skills has been recently introduced at vocational education conferences. At the First Annual Microcomputers in vocational Education Conference in Madison, Wisconsin in 1982, a collection of papers addressing a very wide range of topics was distributed in a handbook. Some of the papers reflect a revaluation of vocational education courses in view of the availability of computer-based tools. It does not appear, however, that vocational educators have participated in anywhere near the number of local, regional, and national conferences on computer-related issues that have been attend by their counterparts in academic education.

Teacher training. The previously cited study by Kapp and Knickerbocker found that nearly every state or territory had made an effort to provide some information on microcomputers to its vocational educators. The sessions lasted from one-half hour to sixty hours and were held on the local, district, regional, and state levels. No information is available on the number of teachers who have received such training or information.

An example of state-supported teacher training is the case of the Vocational Education Services at Indiana University. A series of two-day microcomputer workshops was conducted in the summer and fall of 1984 for vocational educators and administrators. The Vocational Education Services received a fourteen-month grant from the state to become a computer-literacy training centre for teachers in six Indian countries.

Textbooks. One popular textbook in word processing takes a systems approach to office automation by teaching concepts as well as analytic methodology. It addresses the process of change in offices and teaches how to mange all aspects of change. If such a textbook were used in combination with hands-on experience with a variety of office automation equipment, procedures, and tasks, it would seen that the resulting course of instruction would provide the student with a solid understanding of office information processing.

Software developments. During the past four or five years, education and software publishers have been investing heavily in the development and marketing of software aimed at school markets. Until recently, very few of these products have been specifically for vocational education curricula. It appears that educational publishers have not seen vocational education as a ready

market for specially designed software or courseware. This of course will change as the market becomes more apparent.

Computer literacy in vocational education. vocational education must be headed toward a functional integration of technology as well as strong basic skills in communication, information handling, and problem solving. If it is not, the curricula will be hopelessly obsolete. The danger to vocational education is that the traditional separation of computer- related occupational curricula will continue to serve as a model for isolation of computer-related skills and knowledge into separate courses. However, the increasing pressures placed on vocational education programs by industry, the popular press, and parents, and the rapid developments in appropriate application software makes such continued isolation unlikely.

Policy issues for vocational education

The most pervasive problems vis-a-vis the computer revolution and vocational education are the pace of technological and occupational change in the workplace and the inability of traditional vocational education mechanisms and institutions to be proactive with respect to envisioned future requrements. That is, curricula tend to reflect past rather than future workplace requirements.

Budgeting priorities for change. One important reason for th obsolescence of vocational education curricula is that the schools do not budget for change. Vocational education institutions, both secondary and postsecondary, spend a relatively miniscule proportion of their budgets on program development and improvement. Nearly all of their budget goes for maintenance of existing programs. According to a 1979-80 survey, 74 percent of vocational education institutions at the secondary level spent nothing on new programs, and 90 percent spent less than 5 percent of their budget for new services.

The need for current emerging job tasks information. Another problem confronting vocational educators is a lack of current and predictive information regarding the computer-related tasks that will soon be performed by job incumbents in the increasingly automated offices, farms, and factories. Lacking some systematic and accurate basis for reassessing curricula, vocational educators run the risk of investing very large amounts of time and money in developing curricula and operating programs to teach obsolete or low-priority skills and knowledge.

The need for increased focus on cognitive skills and knowledge. Current approaches to analyzing and cataloging job tasks are almost completely behavioral. To gain more insight into the computer-related skills and knowledge needed in many jobs situations, job/task analysis should focus more on cognitive aspects of the task, such as analysis, decision making, troubleshooting, and problem solving. The need for this increased focus on cognitive processes arises from the increasing amounts and kinds of information handling that must be accomplished in most jobs. To understand this point, it is helpful to consider the

characteristics of the information society in contrast to characteristics of the industrial society.

Relative emphasis on emerging versus traditional occupation areas. Current literature in vocational education and the popular press reflect considerable interest in and concern about developing new vocational programs for so-called "emerging" high-technology occupations such as robotics technician and telecommunications specialists. however, the changing roles and tasks of the more traditional occupations are far more important in terms of the actual numbers of students and jobholders who will be affected. Curricula in these basic and traditional vocational areas need to be reassessed in relation to need of the information-based workplace. Computer-based tools and methods, for example, should be integrated into the regular curriculum in all subjects, rather than being isolated as a separate subject of study.

Computer-related skills of students entering vocational education programs. Despite differing perspectives and purposes, nearly every recent educational study group and most state education agencies have recommended that computer literacy be included as one of the "basic" in a core educational curriculum and that increased emphasis be placed on higher-level cognitive and social skills in problem solving and information handling. If the trend toward mandated computer literacy at the junior high school level continues, one would expect students entering vocational education programs to have a variety of skills and knowledge related to computers, which should be taken into account in redesigning programs.

Taking responsibility Economists, sociologists, and futurists disagree in their predictions of the eventual impact of technology and the information age on occupations and skills of workers. But rarely in these discussions is it pointed out that the future is a matter of societal choice and values. As Levin and Rumberger note" "It is clear that application of high technology can be used to enhance the quality of working life and the utilization of workers skills, or to reduce them".

What are appropriate roles for vocation educators in making these choices. From a policy stand-point it would seem appropriate at least to encourage dialogue on an overriding and vital issue. Should educators create a vision of a desirable future and design educational programs around that vision? Or should they wait until industry implements new models and then reactively install educational programs to meet those demands?

Index

Academic programmes, 88

Courses specific to micro computers in education, 88

Contributions to under-graduate courses, 91

Cooperation with other teaching units, 92

Project experience, 90

Advanced research projects agency network, 27

Aids, problem solving, 134

Bell, Daniel, 263

Book literacy, history of, 34

Bibliographic retrieval service, 283

Bord, Alfred, 231

Book literacy, 23

Classrooms, management of, 221

Computer assisted learning, deciding, 199

Level of decision-making, 199

Macro decision, 199

Computer assisted testing, 153

Computer-based on line testing, 154

Computer-based automation, 303

Computer-based learning, 139, 201

Computer bullet in Boards, 283

Computer curriculum, 61, 231

Current developments, flood of, 280

Computer development, stages of, 264

Computer education, 41, 101

Computing, education activities, 61

Computing literacy, 63

Computers and language arts, 64

Computer education, future of, 53

Computer education, current situation, 44

Computers, educational programme, 95, 262

Computers education promise of, 233

Computer education, resource centre, 97

Computers education, study field of, 139

Computer literacy, provincial concept, 28

Computer learning, research use of, 179
Computer literacy, 1, 40
Computer literacy, diverse meanings of, 2
  instrumental literacy, 5
  literacy as algorithmic reasoning,7
  operational literacy, 3
Computer literacy, definition of, 1
Computer learning, instrument for, 146
Computer-managed instruction, 146
  stand-alone dedicated systems, 148
Computer literacy, equal learning opportunity, 20
Computer, organisation learning of, 3, 202
Computer software, analysis, of, 118

Dialogue tutorial CAI, 167
Database inquiry, 172
  global library, 173
  drill and practice, 55
  jackpot, 159
  odd man out, 188
Electronic information exchange system, 283
Ershov, A.P., 7

Higher-order thinking, computers role of, 38, 102
Higher-order thinking, definition of, 102
Higher technology education project of, 310

Information handling systems, 315

Learning through programming, 175
Learning interactions, kinds of, 216
Future implications, 221
Logo research, 216
Lenin and Rumberger's, 4, 303
Literacy education, altered roles for, 10
Literacy, patterns throughout of, 32
LOGO, benefits of, 196
LOGO, origins, 177
LOGO, Piagetion, 198

Manns, Horace, 26
Mendel's laws, 191
Micro computers in classroom, 48
Microcomputer laboratory, 44
Microelectronic technologies, 2
Munford leueis, 238

National Society for Promotion of Industrial Education, 250

Organisation learning, classrooms, in, 204

Papert, Seymour, 8
Programming languages, 137
Problem-solving simulations, 12

Satellites, 29
School of education, 41, 45

Secretarial occupations, requirements for, 313
Simon Herbert, 231
Student learning, monitoring/assessment of, 225

Telecommunication media, 29
Teachers activities, computers for, 85
    computer education and teacher, 86
    role for school of education, 86
    resource of the college and universities, 87
    focus on school and community resources, 85
Turkle, Sherry, 17

Vocational education, defined, 298
Vocational education, computer literacy status of, 318
Vocational education, policy issue for, 323
Vocational education, technology related occupations, 308

World Future Society, 34

